Think Like a Migrant Act Like a Local

by

Goutam Basak

to … Pallabi, Payoja & Girisha

Acknowledgments

This book would not have been possible without the many people who extended their selfless support, who shared their experiences and knowledge with me and pushed me to write this book.

The major influences in my life are the places where I have lived, my family, colleagues, business associates, childhood friends from India and multinational friends in Australia who have been a support to me.

I dedicate this book to all of them who showed me many other dimensions of life. If this book inspires at least one life onto the right track, all the hard work and effort will have been worth it.

Goutam Basak

Contents

Foreword

Around the world and in our own communities, people move in and out of places every day, as they have done throughout human history. Their patterns of movement reflect the conditions of an ever-changing world and in turn, impact the cultural landscapes of the places they leave and the places they settle in ways that often last well beyond their own lifetimes. These imprints on a region include its ethnic make-up, spoken languages, religious institutions, traditions, architectural styles, local food, music, clothes, and other cultural markers.

A family, which is a social cell, is extremely protective about their own interests and susceptible from invasion of outer cultures, values and believes. This mentality is same for a tiny group or a number of several millions of people. Same susceptibility works against migrants as well. Debates have been going on for ages as to whether migration is good for a nation or not.

In reality wherever you see there is growth today you can always find a strong history of migration, because in the background migrants contribute immensely to civic culture, economic growth and prosperity. All migrants, regardless of their status and background, share one crucial characteristic: they uprooted themselves and chose to make a new land their home.

It's an act of courage; moving to a different land with a different culture and norms can be quite daunting, the potential loneliness suffered is not always easy to overcome, and there may be the additional pressure to earn enough to live. I am a migrant and a big supporter of them because of their psychological journey, living with resilience and hope in the new land. With all these they are risk takers, entrepreneurial and one step ahead to become more successful.

Today human movement is a regular phenomenon. New migrants becoming citizens of the new land settling down, taking up jobs and voting in elections. They contribute to bridging skills gaps and bring energy and innovation; host countries are getting enriched by cultural diversity, facilitating growth in tourism, contributing to new ideas helping to grow international trade. Ultimately culture does not mean any individual or collective thing, it means human culture, something greater and shared by all of us—the possibility of participation.

This seeking and open mindset in the new environment when they first arrive helps migrants tackle any opportunity. But in the journey time and time again they get stuck, become comfort seekers and end up in a life which they endure rather than enjoy. The zeal and hunger to make their lives better is lost somewhere. They have to remind themselves it was their choice to migrate to achieve their dreams so integration and assimilation in the host culture is crucial. Simultaneously understanding the cultural difference, rule of life, and perspective of viewing things are always better for both parties to work collaboratively and achieve the optimum result—and for this reason that "Think like a migrant, act like a local" is relevant in today's globalized, diverse, hyper connected world.

Goutam Basak

Goutam Basak

x

CHAPTER 1

Why - Think like a Migrant

"Remember, remember always, that all of us, and you and I especially, are descended from immigrants and revolutionists."
Franklin D. Roosevelt

Diversity and multiculturalism are the hot topics of discussion nowadays, and migrants are the living examples of multiculturalism. Glenn Llopis wrote in his Harvard Business Review article "If you want to remain relevant and advance your career in today's global marketplace, you need to serve as an enabler of business growth and innovation. One of the best ways to do this is to adopt an 'immigrant mindset.'"

The idea for this book was conceptualized long ago but I did not find enough courage to go ahead with it. In my first book I wrote forty articles uncovering insights into the four quadrants of life:

- Human - everything in the world is by us, to us, for us.
- Migration - human migration and the cultural mix, a global topic.
- Mental health and well-being - just as vital as physical health, whole person healing is the new medical science.
- Commerce - social responsibility, giving back, building lives are the mantra in this capitalistic society.

In this book, I will only focus on human migration. I have strong feelings and beliefs that migration is a great thing for any land and migrants are already psychologically half way ahead to succeeding. An interesting report titled "Partnership for a new American economy" echoed the same feeling.[1]

---

[1] http://www.renewoureconomy.org

According to a study titled the "new American", more than 40% of Fortune 500 companies operating in 2010 were founded by immigrants or their children—including some of the most well-known brands, from Apple and IBM to Disney and McDonalds. The companies noted in this study had combined revenues of $4.2 trillion—more than the GDP of most countries.

World Migration

Global migration has increased immensely in the last ten years and it is rising every day. In October 2013 a joint contribution by the United Nations Department of Economic and Social Affairs (UN-DESA) and the Organization for Economic Co-operation and Development (OECD) confirmed "Some 232 million international migrants are living in the world today. Since 1990, the number of international migrants in the global North increased by around 53 million (65%), while the migrant population in the global South grew by around 24 million (34%). Today, about six out of every ten international migrants reside in the developed regions." Intra-country or intrastate human movement data are not well tracked, though we know a lot of human migration happens and is occurring from villages to city.

The below table shows world inter-country migration in figures:[2]

International Migrant Stock (Millions) (1990-2013)

Source: United Nations, Department of Economic and Social Affairs (2013). Trends in International Migrant Stock: The 2013 Revision-Migrants by Age and Sex.

	1990	2000	2010	2013
World	154.2	174.5	220.7	231.5
Developed regions	82.3	103.4	129.7	135.6
Developing regions	71.9	71.1	91	95.9
Africa	15.6	15.6	17.1	18.6
Asia	49.9	50.4	67.8	70.8
Europe	49	56.2	69.2	72.4
LAC (Latin America and the Caribbean)	7.1	6.5	8.1	8.5
NA (Northern America)	27.8	40.4	51.2	53.1
Oceania	4.7	5.4	7.3	7.9

During the 1990s, the global migrant stock grew at an average of about 2 million migrants per year. The decade 2000-10 saw the growth in the migrant stock accelerate to about 4.6 million migrants annually—twice as fast than during the previous decade.

So the risk taking abilities, power to adapt to the new environment and zeal to learn new ways of life give these migrants lots of cutting edge and a core attitude for survival. This nature of competition, adaptation and change help to grow the whole community, state and ultimately the whole nation.

Another interesting report, "They came, they conquered" by Stephen Lacey 3 also aligns

---

[2] http://www.oecd.org/els/mig/World-Migration-in-Figures.pdf
[3] The Sydney Morning Herald April 23, 2013

with my point of view. In that article Lacey wrote about migrants who found outstanding success: "...with almost 25 per cent of Australian current population born overseas, and a recent US study suggesting that migrants are four times more likely to become self-made millionaires."

Three Global Migrant Success Stories

Elon Musk was born in Pretoria, Transvaal, South Africa. After his parents divorced in 1980, Musk lived mostly with his father in South Africa. He taught himself computer programming and at age 12 sold the code for a BASIC-based video game he created called Blastar to a magazine called PC and Office Technology for approximately US$500. He was severely bullied throughout his childhood, and was once hospitalized when a group of boys threw him down a flight of stairs and then beat him until he blacked out. After graduating from the University of Pennsylvania he moved to California to begin a PhD in applied physics at Stanford University but left the program after two days to pursue his entrepreneurial aspirations in the areas of the internet, renewable energy and outer space. After an initial few ups and downs in the journey he is now the founder, CEO and CTO of SpaceX, co-founder, CEO and product architect of Tesla Motors, chairman of SolarCity, co-chairman of OpenAI, co-founder of Zip2, and co-founder of PayPal. As of January 2016, he has an estimated net worth of US$12.4 billion.

Lakshmi Mittal was born in Sadulpur, Rajasthan, India. At the age of 6 he migrated with his family to Kolkata, India, as in the villages there was not much promise to live a decent life. He was brought up in a middle class migrant family in a small flat in central Kolkata. He graduated from St. Xavier's College, Kolkata with a bachelor degree in Commerce. His family started a steel business in Kolkata and bought land in Indonesia due to the curb of steel production by the Indian government. In 1976 at the age of 26 Lakshmi went to Indonesia to sell the land because nothing was happening. He then decided to start his journey as he sensed an opportunity in the steel business due to the prevailing free economic policy. He then took over Mexican company Trinidad. He is chairman and CEO of ArcelorMittal, the world's largest steelmaking company. He lives in London as one of the richest and most respected entrepreneurs in the world—still holding his Indian citizenship and passport.

Sergey Brin was born in Moscow, Russia, when it was still part of the Soviet Union and was compelled to migrate to the United States when he was six years old. Sergey's father explains how he was "forced to abandon his dream of becoming an astronomer even before he reached college." Because of political unrest, the Brin family formally applied for their exit visa in September 1978, and, as a result, his father was fired and his mother had to leave her job. For the next eight months, without any steady income, they were forced to take on temporary jobs as they waited for their request which would be denied, as it was for many refuseniks. The term "refusenik" is derived from the "refusal" handed down to a prospective emigrant from the Soviet authorities. During this time his parents shared responsibility for looking after him and his father taught himself computer programming. In May 1979, they were granted their official exit visas and were allowed to leave the country. In an interview in October 2000, Brin said, "I know the hard times that my parents went through there and am very thankful that I was brought to the States." During an orientation for new students at Stanford, he met Larry Page. Together they founded Google in 1998.

Three Australian Migrant Success Stories

Frank Lowy spent part of his childhood in a detention camp in Cyprus and a detainee camp in Palestine. He joined his family in Australia in 1952 and—along with John Saunders another Hungarian immigrant—developed his first shopping centre at Blacktown in Sydney in 1959. Nowadays, the Westfield Group operates as one of the world's largest shopping centre portfolios with 104 shopping malls across the world.

Richard Pratt was born in the Free City of Danzig (modern Gdańsk), Poland of Polish Jewish parents in 1934. His family immigrated to Australia in 1938 and settled in Shepparton, Victoria. Pratt played for Carlton in the Victorian Football League's (VFL) under-19s competition. Pratt took over the family packaging business Visy (founded by his father) after his father's death in 1969. His net worth when he died in 2009 was more than $5 billion.

Harry Triguboff known as "High-Rise Harry",

was born in Russia and forced to escape from northern China during Lenin's ascendancy. He arrived in Australia in 1947 at the age of 14. After finishing his education in textiles, he worked in South Africa and Israel in the textile business. On returning to Australia in 1960, Triguboff took a while to find his feet. He worked as a taxi driver, a milkman and a real estate agent. He bought a block of land in Tempe in Sydney on which he built a block of eight units, which led to his Eureka moment. His next development project comprised 18 units on a block in Meriton Street, Gladesville. He revolutionised the way Australians live. He founded Meriton in 1963 which is now Australia's biggest residential apartment development company.

Three Intra-country Success Stories

Dhirubhai Ambani was born in Chorvad, Junagadh State, British Raj (now Gujarat, India) then migrated to Yemen and earned money by working with a firm in the 1950s, moving to Mumbai in 1958 to start his own business in spices. After making modest profits, he moved into textiles. The first office of the Reliance Commercial Corporation was set up at the Narsinatha Street in Masjid Bunder. It was a 350 sq ft (33 m2) room with a telephone, one table and three chairs. Initially, the entrepreneur had two assistants to help with the business. During this period, Ambani and his family stayed in a two-bedroom apartment at the Jai Hind Estate in Bhuleshwar, Mumbai. Extensive marketing of the brand in India made it a household name. Franchise retail outlets were started and they sold the "Only Vimal" brand of textiles. Now the company has nearly 100,000 employees and is listed among the Fortune 500 companies.

Sir Ka-shing Li was born in Chaozhou, Guangdong, China in 1928 and is now a Hong Kong business magnate, investor, philanthropist and one of the most powerful figures in Asia. Li was named "Asia's Most Powerful Man" by Asia Week in 2001. Due to his father's death, he was forced to leave school before the age of 15 and found a job in a plastics trading company where he labored 16 hours a day. By 1950 he was able to start his own company, Cheung Kong Industries. From manufacturing plastics, Li developed his company into a leading real estate investment company in Hong Kong that was listed on the Hong Kong Stock Exchange in 1972. Li is also regarded as one of Asia's most generous philanthropists having donated to date over US$1.41 billion to charity and other various philanthropic causes.

Mark Zuckerberg was born in White Plains, New York, USA and brought up in Dobbs Ferry, New York, a small town about 10 miles north of New York City. His parents were originally from Bulgaria. After finishing school he went to Harvard and with a couple of friends launched Facebook from his Harvard dormitory room on February 4, 2004 as "Thefacebook" (originally thefacebook.com). He moved to Palo Alto, California with some friends and leased a small house that served as an office. They planned to return to Harvard but eventually decided to remain in California. Since 2010, Mark Zuckerberg has been named among Time magazine's 100 wealthiest and most influential people in the world.

When in Rome, Do as the Romans Do

According to Kauffman Foundation research migrants were almost twice as likely to start businesses in 2012 as native-born, nearly 30% of new entrepreneurs in 2014 were migrants and about one-quarter of the engineering and technology companies started between 2006–

2012 had at least one key founder who was a migrant in the USA. I am sure this positive trend is the same in other parts of the world.

There are numerous success stories like these who came and conquered but simultaneously there are millions of unsuccessful stories where either they had to go back home or are living unwillingly in a foreign land with lots of unhappiness. From my research I found a general physician back home ultimately worked in a packaging industry in the new land throughout her life; a well-regarded engineer in his own country worked as a taxi driver for life; a well-educated and experienced researcher in science who ended up as a receptionist and so on. For a small time just to survive, we have to do many things we are not comfortable with but that doesn't mean it will shred our dream, our motivation, our real inner core and our beliefs.

Though there are lots of uncertainties for settlement, migrants have a tremendous hope inside them that this movement actually solved some of their problems in lives and is a major step towards achieving their dream. This attitude makes them more adaptable to the new environment. Locals (not everyone) on the other hand predominantly are comfort seekers compared with migrants. Their status, respect, culture and community are more important aspects than going out in the world to make some changes. But please note this: when these locals become migrants instantly their mindset and behavior change overnight.

Competition is one of the most basic functions of nature. It remains a powerful instinctual drive in humans. We compete for resources in the forms of food, jobs, living quarters and general status in society. We compete against each other; we compete against ourselves, and we compete as groups against other groups. Migrants in many cases adopt local language, lifestyle and habits quickly for the strong need of acceptance and achieving social status and way of life.

Migrants always lift population, participation and productivity—for high economic growth. This book will help those who feel stuck and want to get out of this discomfort and failure zone to make changes in their lives. I will not be using the term "immigrant" or "emigrant" but profoundly saying "Migrants". Migration is a movement.

Thinking like migrants is relevant in today's

multicultural world. But as we know from the saying "when in Rome, do as the Romans do", we have to act a certain way or to be very precise: act like a local. Don't get me wrong, I am not saying forget your culture or values; it's just those local norms, beliefs, way of life and so on. This book will give you insights into the phases that every migrant goes through, an understanding of what to look for and will provide a road map to handle the situations which some find hard to cope with or adjust to. Above all in this hyper connected and mobile world, understanding different cultures, human behavior and others' perspective are become a necessity for both the hosts and migrants. That's why I name this book "Think like a migrant, act like a local."

CHAPTER 2

Dislocation - From Known to Unknown

"If you can't fly then run, if you can't run then walk, if you can't walk then crawl, but whatever you do you have to keep moving forward."
Martin Luther King Jr.

What Is Migration?

Migration, for humans, is the movement of people from one place to another. People can choose to move or are forced to move for various reasons. Since pre-historic times, people have moved for food, shelter and safety. Though in our current world people do it for education, employment, economy, health, relationship, political and civil reasons, safety, and so on. Migration can occur in different ways and can be inter-country or intra-country.

Types of Migration[4]

Internal Migration: Moving to a new home within a state, country, or continent.

External Migration: Moving to a new home in a different state, country, or continent.

Emigration: Leaving one country to move to another (e.g., the Pilgrims emigrated from England).

Immigration: Moving into a new country (e.g., the Pilgrims immigrated to America).

Population Transfer: When a government forces a large group of people out of a region, usually based on ethnicity or religion. This is also known as an involuntary or forced migration.

---

[4]http://www.nationalgeographic.com/migrationguidestudent.pdf

Impelled Migration (also called "reluctant" or "imposed" migration): Individuals are not forced out of their country, but leave because of unfavorable situations such as warfare, political problems, or religious persecution.

Step Migration: A series of shorter, less extreme migrations from a person's place of origin to final destination—such as moving from a farm to a village, to a town, and finally to a city.

Chain Migration: A series of migrations within a family or defined group of people. A chain migration often begins with one family member who sends money to bring other family members to the new location. Chain migration results in migration fields—the clustering of people from a specific region into certain neighborhoods or small towns.

Return Migration: The voluntary movements of immigrants back to their place of origin. This is also known as circular migration.

Seasonal Migration: The process of moving for a period of time in response to labor or climate conditions (e.g., farm workers following crop harvests or working in cities off-season;

"snowbirds" moving to the southern and southwestern United States during winter).

People Who Migrate

Emigrant: A person who is leaving a country to reside in another.

Immigrant: A person who is entering a country from another to take up new residence.

Refugee: A person who is residing outside the country of his or her origin due to fear of persecution for reasons of race, religion, nationality, membership in a particular social group, or political opinion.

Internally Displaced Person (IDP): A person who is forced to leave his or her home region because of unfavorable conditions (political, social, environmental, etc.) but does not cross any boundaries. The UN estimates there are 42.5 million people displaced by persecution and conflict around the world.

Migration Stream: A group migration from a particular country, region, or city to a certain destination.
People migrate for different reasons but it

mainly comes down to two things: firstly, leaving a place because of some problems, and secondly, moving to a place because of better promises or hope.

Impacts of Migration

Human migration affects population patterns and characteristics, social and cultural patterns and processes, economies, and physical environments. As people move, their cultural traits and ideas diffuse along with them, creating and modifying cultural landscapes.

Diffusion: The process through which certain characteristics (e.g., cultural traits, ideas, disease) spread over space and through time.

Relocation Diffusion: Ideas, cultural traits, etc. that move with people from one place to another and do not remain in the point of origin.

Expansion Diffusion: Ideas, cultural traits, etc., that move with people from one place to another but are not lost at the point of origin, such as language.

Cultural markers: Structures or artifacts (e.g.,

buildings, spiritual places, architectural styles, signs, etc.) that reflect the cultures and histories of those who constructed or occupy them.

The Pre-migration Phase

In the pre-migration phase when we are exploring ideas and opportunities to leave our home land, we always have various questions in our mind: the problems, issues we want to leave behind, the dream we want to achieve and so on. With our personal knowledge, peer or family influence and different opportunities, we figure out where should we migrate and how—the destination and the strategy.

We all know in the bottom of our heart that we want to migrate to find the solutions to one or a combination of problems and issues hindering smooth progress in our existing life, such as:

- **Economic problem** - financial stability and better future economic prospects
- **Social problem** - better standard of living.
- **Educational problem** - better opportunity for professional / higher education
- **Political problem** - relief from political unrest situation upsetting life's equilibrium

- **Family problem** - settling of some disharmony in the family.

Boom, then one day, the migrant sets his foot on the soil of his chosen land—his mind filled to the brim with the golden dreams of a new innings in his life.

Post-migration Phases

During adaptation, in the new land with its unfamiliar inhabitants nurturing an alien culture in an unknown environment, speaking a strange language (in some cases a known language with a different accent), following an altogether different set of norms, codes of conduct and rules, every one of the migrants goes through different stages of physical, physiological and psychological cycles. Some of them struggle to adjust while some others embrace it gladly from the very first day. From a mental orientation perspective, either accepting it or rejecting it they all go through the same phases of ups and downs.

We often describe it as some sort of *culture shock*. This happens due to changes in perceptions, value systems, rules of life and way of living and style of communication.

Kalvero Oberg first identified different phases of culture shock.

The Four Phase Cycle (4Rs) [5]
1. Rejoicing Phase
2. Rejection Phase
3. Regression Phase
4. Recovery Phase

1. The Rejoicing Phase

This is the honeymoon period or the "selfie phase." Migrants arrive with great expectations and a positive mindset. They are on their way to making a better living, chasing their dream and leaving behind problems they had in their home land. They are in a fully seeking and open mindset, exploring and observing every detail of the society.

In this phase they always try to find the bright side of the coin. Tolerance levels remain extended and there is excitement, new sights, smells, tastes and anything new appears as intriguing and exciting. Normal perceptions we all have in this phase are that life will be better from the first day, opportunities are waiting and

---

[5] http://www.lossesintranslation.com/stages-of-immigration.php

we will get a lot of time and support from others. With this kind of joy in mind and happiness in the brain, we perceive all these hurdles as normal challenges and endeavor to overcome them successfully. A few typical examples are finding information about public transport, food, accommodation, communication, banking, medical facilities and schooling.

- Excitement with new sounds, sights, smells.
- Superficial involvement in the host culture (like a tourist).
- Intrigue with both similarities and differences between the new culture and home culture.
- Lots of interest in learning, very motivated and cooperative.
- Feel as if you will be able to handle anything—"I am not going to have any problems adjusting!"

In today's world thanks to the internet we have all the necessary information at our fingertips. But information and experiences are not the same.

2. The Rejection Phase

Everything has an end and in that way the Rejoicing phase has its own warranties. Newcomers now start facing the rule of life slowly. Your perception about this new land now starts undergoing a change. You now start comparing the new land with your previous experiences.

Seems like people somehow no longer care about your problems. In fact it is not because they don't want to support you, rather they don't have enough time or your concern isn't a priority at that given point of time. And then you start thinking that the people in your new land don't like newcomers and you may begin to feel aggressive and start to complain about the new culture and country. **It is important to recognize that these feelings are real and can become acute.**

This phase is mentally very challenging because maybe you have been unemployed in the new land for six months, or you are missing your family or your daily leisure. This is where migrants start rejecting the host land in every respect. Either you get stronger and bounce back or you get weaker physically and mentally.

Migration always happens because of pull and push factors. Push factors such as not enough jobs, fewer opportunities, inadequate conditions, natural calamities, political and religious reasons, poor medical care, loss of wealth, poor living conditions, bullying and discrimination. Pull factors are better opportunities, better living conditions, more freedom, education, better medical care, climates, security and more industry. In this phase, all the push factors become faded and migrants don't enjoy the pull factors.

- The novelty of the new culture has worn off, and you now focus primarily on the *differences* between the new culture and your home culture.
- Small differences feel like major catastrophes. You become overly concerned with and stressed out by problems and feel helpless and frustrated.
- Stereotypes and prejudices surface: you feel as if the host nationals are cold, unhelpful, snobbish.
- You search out local friends.

- You are homesick. You miss your friends and family.

3. The Regression Phase

The next phase is the Regression phase. Here mentally they go back to the home land. All those problems which gave them pain and discomfort become oblivious and it is now about remembering the brighter side of the old land.

In this phase you spend much of your time speaking your own language, watching videos from your home country, eating traditional food. Without realizing, you start moving in social circles which are exclusively made up of people from your own background and you don't want to meet locals. This becomes inevitable when you have a severe language problem. They just don't prefer to be with the locals, to find comfort and acceptance they end up living and dealing with their own community.

Here you have to think of the very reasons for which you are in this new land and with your own mindset you are blocking one major aspect of it—to get the full benefit from this new environment.

In this phase, migrants spend most of the social time complaining about the new culture and its strange and senseless ways. The drawbacks in the home land seem wonderful; in extreme cases you may find yourself wondering why you ever left. You may now only remember your home country as a wonderful place in which nothing ever went wrong for you.

- You are becoming more familiar with the new culture and its "logic" and values. Cultural cues become easier to read.

- You feel more comfortable and less isolated, and you even begin to prefer some aspects of the new culture to your home culture.

- You feel like "As long as I am here, I should make the most of it."

- You experience periodic personal highs and lows, as adjustment gradually takes place.

- Your sense of humor returns. You are able to laugh at certain ways of doing things that previously just annoyed you and even to laugh at yourself from time to time.

- Since you are past the initial, emotional stages of cultural adjustment, you can now enter a stage of "deeper learning." You begin to see a multitude of approaches to your life abroad and to question some of your assumptions about the world. This can be both exciting and unnerving.

4. The Recovery Phase

After all the psychological drama you start saying to yourself enough is enough. Then you reach the Recovery phase. The pain, suffering and hardship you have gone through mentally in this new land you now realise makes no sense, you start becoming more comfortable with the land and you also feel more comfortable with the customs of your new land. Your feeling of insecurity, fear of unknown and preoccupied mind about illusive thoughts from your own country starts fading.

You are well equipped now to embrace it. Your judgments are getting clearer and you start to realize that no country is that much better than another—it is just different lifestyles and different ways of dealing with the problems of life. With this new adjustment, you start accepting the food, drinks, habits and customs. You now understand that there are different ways to live your life and that no way is really better than another, just different. Finally, you become comfortable in the new place.

- The "new" culture is no longer new; instead, the "foreign" land you live in now feels like another home.
- The aspects of the culture that are different no longer affect you in a negative way. You are able to live and work to your full potential.
- Just like your homeland, you appreciate certain aspects of the foreign culture and are critical of others.

A few interesting findings during research:

- We might perceive that the transition for same language speaking people to adjust in another country is easier, but it's a similar experience that everyone goes through.
- Does the color of your skin make a difference? No. Maybe it used to matter a few decades ago but not now in this progressive world. But not speaking the local language definitely matters.

Everyone tries to find their own community during the initial phases of settlement. But many people confine themselves in that and do not want to come out because of fear and comfort.

So understand the stages of cultural adjustment, analyze your situations and reactions; be flexible; tolerate ambiguity; expect things can be different and the optimum approach. Be patient; don't try to understand everything immediately; identify what helps you manage stress, thinking positively, give yourself permission to fail.

This is the time you again come back to your own self; you start dealing again with your own passion, zeal and motivation. People start playing the instrument they used to play, start indulging in the sports they love, start going to local festivals, and mingle more and more in this new land. Everyone experiences all the phases not necessarily in the same time span or magnitude. It may vary, but roughly it takes two to four years to feel fully settled. It depends on so many other factors such as your duration of stay, your family support system, your commitment, your own situation, your power of will and so on. But all these come down to one and only one thing—**YOU**.

CHAPTER 3

Being to Becoming

"People come here penniless but not cultureless. They bring us gifts. We can synthesize the best of our traditions with the best of theirs. We can teach and learn from each other to produce a better place."
Mary Pipher, **psychologist and author**

We all sacrifice some things to achieve other things. However, we shouldn't regard those as sacrifices rather take them as the preparation for the big show. Wellness authority Greg Anderson has said "Focus on the journey, not the destination. Joy is found not in finishing an activity but in doing it."

I have seen many international students who would study in the university the whole day and work the whole night in warehouses for sheer survival. A Chinese friend of mine, Xin was compelled to follow this lifestyle to subsist. Ultimately, he finished his study with distinction and now despite his inadequate command over English, he is working in a multinational company as technical head with 30 professionals reporting to him. I am sure there are many migrants with the same story.

Migrants' Two Challenges

When you come to your chosen new land it comes down to two major things:

- initial settlement needs when you first arrive
- ongoing challenges in relationships, roles in the community and belonging.

Yes, initial settlement is a major part. When I enquired with those who had already migrated decades ago and then with those who had been migrated for a few years in different places, the majority of them agreed that it normally takes 2 to 4 years to feel settled, to start mobilising the comfort that they belong to this place. By that time, you should find yourself well-positioned amongst members of your own community, you find your own interests and the major reason for your migration well-attended. All migrants everywhere have gone through the same journey.

Don't get me wrong on this because there may be exceptions. It depends on the individual and their own circumstances and mindset. In some cases, even after migration decades ago, you find people complaining about local things and glorifying some facets of life back home. We are all very much human; we all have our emotions, and we all have our own ways of looking at the world. But if you think logically and try to relate these people to the different stages of migration which were discussed in the last chapter, such people may still be in a phase in between the two extremes.

We know we have to learn the rules of the game

The learning stint starts from the very first hour, post-arrival. In my case, before I came to Australia I had never used a mobile phone or an ATM card in my own homeland. So, after reaching Australia, I had to learn to pick up such habits. Taking advantage of this learning mechanism, some migrants develop the regular habit of reading local business or sports magazines according to their personal likings. Some of them choose to attend the local free events and this is where they meet other migrants with similar interests. Just to survive (as we all know—crisis is the mother of invention), the migrants look out for and try to identify some opportunities to earn. The job choices include cleaning households, gardens, sea beaches, offices, factories, stores and shopping malls and serving or washing dishes in restaurants and cafes, housekeeping. The migrants who take up such assignments, if they are from the third world, would not have ever imagined performing such jobs in their homelands as back home they would be from middle and upper middle class families where such services come from local unskilled workers on small payments.

We know we have to be smart

In the host country, only a handful of migrants may do great things from the very first day but most of the fresher's happen to choose a more conventional approach which can generate money from day one: they seek out potential opportunities everywhere and at every moment.

A typical migrant attitude and behavior is to have a "fire in the belly" from the very first day to prove his worth and to show folks back home, "Yes I have made it." They know very well that they have to be smart and find economic avenues.

We know no one will hear our sad story

An average migrant goes through stages of progressive development and the process may not imply prestige and status for almost two-thirds or three-quarters of the journey. Migrants ought to treat it not as a problem but as a challenge. One migrant from Iran, that I came across during my research, who had been working in a workshop said "I used to sleep on the warehouse floor so that next morning I can start early and get more money." He would never imagine doing this in his homeland as there he will fall from his status and obviously lose face to his fellow men. But in a foreign land, he could do it unhesitatingly as there was nobody to see who he was and in a first world country there is no class distinction between one job and another. Every job is considered an economic pursuit and so social, cultural or religious flavor would not be associated with it. Taking up any economic occupation, irrespective of its nature, to earn a livelihood— all migrants do it, keep their mouth shut and just work with no embarrassment, self-pity or sense of guilt while slowly working their way up.

We know we can overcome all odds and work with a genuine purpose

When a newcomer lands on foreign soil and tries to tell his story immediately we, the old migrants, comment: "We have all gone through this, it's nothing new for us." Whenever we, the old timers, try to prove our better worth compared to the newcomers, we say: "We came with just a few bucks in our pocket and a suitcase and look where we are today; look at our standard of living."

The old migrants set glorious goals for themselves and witness sunny dreams, and then work really hard to reach such destinations and realize the visions and, in the process, really prove that they set foot on alien soil with nothing and have established their worth by enhancing an enviable standard of living. So they come to believe that they can overcome all odds whatever comes to make their life worth living.

Only uprooted people can truly appreciate the importance of roots. The sense of place, belonging and deep familiarity are missing from daily life and must be recreated to feel whole again. Some of the migrants have little to no money, and they barely speak the local language. But still they do well. If you dig a bit deeper, it makes a lot of sense.

- They come not to do what they love. They are here to make their lives better, to prosper. For economic migrants happiness is in their mind but mostly translated through money. With that money they can provide a better future for their families and, most importantly, provide their children with the things that they never had.

- They don't think in terms of a 40-hour workweek; instead they try to figure out how they can work extra hours each week. Money saved is money earned. This is the normal mentality that makes them frugal.

- When times get tough, the one thing that increases the odds of success is having a good education. This is a survival mindset to involve more into education.

- If the migrants are really inadequate in the local language or professional skills, from a sheer survival mindset, they become self-employed. And that mindset and success follows in the next generations.

An ultimate hunger to become equal with the locals makes them even more ambitious—a go getter, creative, flexible and productive. But again there have been many cases of migrants who were resistant to adapt to the foreign environment and had to give up the hope of settling down. They had no other choice but to return to their homeland. For another migrant, adaptation can be forced where the individual or the family is unwilling to adjust to the circumstances. In some cases, their own identities and socio-cultural norms are so strong they feel lots of stress and anxiety in this acculturation process.

Within the familiar surroundings of the ethnic group, the migrant or minority group member will usually find acceptance, common interests, opportunities to give and receive and a sense of belonging; it gives them ease to adapt in the new land. The experience during the process of their psychological and sociocultural adaptation to the host culture has far-reaching effects in terms of mental health, employment and for the whole society.

Different Patterns of Strategies

There are two distinct patterns linked to acculturation strategies integration and separation. Migrants who experienced high levels of psychological distress in the initial stage of their resettlement, and who later chose the integration strategy of acculturation were more successful and satisfied with their adaptation than those who chose the strategy of separation. The integration strategy worked proved by research and some examples of this are: picking up the local language, dialect, accent, slangs etc., local dress habits, use of accessories, local habits (Friday drink, cycling to work, going to the gym during office lunch hours, weekend sports, different cultural food etc.), getting friendly with members of the local opposite sex and, in some cases, getting married, political knowledge and in some cases picking up the local style of spirituality. We will explain later in detail about acculturation.

All these activities are nothing but finding, molding, accepting, and embracing the new sentiment, the different way of life. Every human being has the necessary intelligence to survive, but to face it in reality and act towards it needs lots of courage and hope and dealing with uncertainties. Living with these uncertainties makes migrants strong, resilient and successful.

Typically in the initial phase migrants and locals deal for business purposes, but they do not intend to develop emotional or meaningful ties with one another. There is observation, curiosity, and mistrust working in the mind. People from both groups are generally cautious about how to act and what to say to one another. They have mixed emotions and are to some extent afraid to open up to strangers. Normal human psyche also works in the same way—susceptible to unknown.

Getting Comfort

Cuban anthropologist Fernando Ortiz describes this as "the reciprocal process, by which two cultures, upon contact, engage in a system of give and take and adaptation to each other's ways, though often not in an equal manner, resulting in the emergence of a new cultural reality."

After frequent meetings, both parties begin to develop emotional ties with one another as well as learn and appreciate each other's culture. On one side as the dominant culture should exert a great deal of patience, humility, understanding, tolerance, and respect for the new group, so should the new group be willing to learn and embrace their new language and culture. Although the established culture is less affected during this transculturation; its norms and values are still impacted to a certain degree by the new culture. But this is the most sensitive stage in multicultural integration. Most conflict and misunderstanding occur here.

What's happening in the migration prone state or countries, if the level of tolerance or adaptation from both the groups is lower than the rapid influx of newcomers—roughly 80% chance that both groups will split into segregated cultural groups or communities? Cultural norms and values of older first-generation migrants remain generally unchanged during this journey but their children who migrated with them undergo significant changes. They absorb new customs and new ways of thinking and doing things through their newly embraced educational system, media, and friends. This often creates tension between different generations. But study shows successful are those who are open-minded, feel accepted and begin to join local community and groups.

It is true that for ethnically segregated cities this integration is very tough but in cities where lots of mixing from different countries and cultures is happening every day, things are much easier. The more open-minded migrants who embrace the new land get the acceptance from locals as they see others' willingness to adjust which basically drills down to more respect. Locals then start inviting migrants to their homes for dinner and holidays, appreciate others' cultural norms and values, allow their children to mix and develop trust and confidence in them. This is truly the way from being to becoming.

CHAPTER 4

Acculturation - Building the Bridge

"You can make more friends in two months by becoming interested in other people than you can in two years by trying to get other people interested in you"
Dale Carnegie

Now let's discuss what the settling down phase looks like. Migrants are very well accustomed with this concept and everyone goes through this process in their own way. Acculturation is the process that occurs when different individuals or groups of people meet and exchange aspects of their culture. Due to advances in transportation, communication, and technology, there has been a significant increase in the interactions among different cultures. For migrants this very psychological process become vital for their own life and future.

For first-generation migrants, for whom acculturation is most difficult due to the lack of precedents in their family, the speed of adaptation varies depending on the individual's interest and motivation. Several types of acculturation are possible as a result of this process:[6]

1. Assimilation: when one desires minimal or no contact with one's culture of origin, and keeps frequent contact with the host culture.

2. Integration: when one keeps high involvement with one's culture of origin, and at the same time has high involvement with the host culture.

---

[6] http://www.newworldencyclopedia.org/entry/Acculturation

3. Separation: when one maintains high involvement with the culture of origin, but prefers minimal involvement with the host culture.

4. Marginalization: when one desires no contact with either one's culture of origin or a host culture.

5. Transmutation: when one decides to identify with a third culture, which is often a combination of both the culture of origin and a host culture.

Inevitably, with each generation, the dominance of host culture gradually becomes the dominant. That's why it takes three generations for migrants to behave typically like a local. Another common, but less lasting effect of individual-level acculturation occurs when a traveler spends some time in a foreign place, away from his or her own culture.

Stages in the Acculturation Process are basically phases of migration. It's a process whereby they become accustomed with the unknown.

- During the first stage initial enthusiasm, excitement, and eagerness, some anxiety about the future but feel optimistic about the new land and new opportunities.

- During the second stage confusion, misunderstandings, anxiety, feel isolated, demonstrate withdrawal, alienation or aggressive behavior, avoidance of mainstream culture or community.

- During the third stage have more constructive attitudes and feel less anxious, try out different local norms, getting comfortable in local language.

- During the fourth stage feel their emotional equilibrium is restored, express humor and trust, learnt to value both old and new cultures.

Acculturation is a process of cultural and psychological change. Its effects can be seen at multiple levels; at the group level, acculturation often results in changes to culture, customs, and social institutions (food, clothing, and language). At the individual level, changes in daily behavior are seen such as beliefs and norms.

Big Factor

One factor that contributes to acculturation is resilience. Resilience is defined as an individual's ability to effectively cope with significant stressors or adverse and threatening situations. It is the ability to "bounce back" to a previous state of normal functioning or using personal strengths and behaviors to avoid negative effects of adversities. Resilience is not a trait, but an ongoing continuous process of using interpersonal and intrapersonal capacities to successfully adapt to life stressors. Personal strengths and resources, cultural and traditional protective factors and practices play a role in the well-being of ethnically diverse individuals. Religious and spiritual beliefs (prayer, meditation, and other rituals) provide a purpose to life and meaning and may contribute to resiliency among migrants.

Acculturative Stress

After moving to a new culture, meeting challenges such as a new language, different customs and laws, distinct norms of social behavior, etc. often brings a certain amount of stress, known as acculturative stress.

Research has shown that acculturative stress is an important factor in the mental health of migrants, as it increases the risk for various psychological problems. Several variables are associated with the degree of acculturative stress. The greater the differences between the two cultures, the higher the stress. The reason for moving to the new culture is a significant factor, as is the degree of receptiveness of the host society.

In the multicultural world in which we now live, acculturation is a process that more and more people experience every day. As the world is becoming one "global village," it is easier than ever to move from one part to another, and to transition from one culture to another. With this constant flux, people become more knowledgeable about different cultures, and at the same time more understanding of cultural differences. Cultures become recognized for their inherent value, as well as for their contribution to diversity in the world. Intercultural identities play an important role in this, bridging the gap between once distant cultures.

Acculturation stress can be an important factor in the mental health of migrants and ethnically diverse groups. Acculturative stress is commonly found among migrants, yet a lot of them do not perceive it as a stress and simply assume that those afflicting feelings will soon be over with time. Sometimes it can turn into social phobia like cognitive anxiety, depression, and even suicide ideation— sufferers should seek help to adapt to the new culture as soon as possible. This requires the efforts of both sufferers and the society, including professionals with specific treatments, as well as other sources of social supports so that migrants can overcome the stressful status and regain confidence.

I think this education is very necessary in the migrants' community so they can extend their hands to those who are in need especially with the culturally and linguistically diverse (CALD) groups. Let's take Australia as an example, but the scenario all over the world is more or less similar.

- Migrants who have had to overcome huge obstacles towards resettlement, experience some sort of torture and trauma, may experience loss, grief, depression, anger, and other emotional difficulties. CALD Australians are susceptible to missing out on mental health services due to language difficulties, different cultural understandings of mental health, cultural stigma, unfamiliarity with the health systems, and the overall lack of culturally competent health services.

- People from CALD backgrounds have a significantly lower level of access to mental health care and support in the wider community, due to stigma, language and cultural issues, resulting in much greater responsibility placed on family members without adequate culturally appropriate support or education.

- CALD consumers tend to access specialist mental health services through emergency hospital departments at a severe or crisis stage of their condition, which prolongs their ill health and decreases quality of life.

- Lack of cultural awareness and understanding in mental health services inhibits early diagnosis.

- Individuals whose primary language and education is not local may have lower levels of acculturation and have an increased risk of developing depression. For them higher levels of social engagement with their culture of origin are associated with a decreased risk of anxiety symptoms.

The experience and extent of acculturative stress is influenced by a number of factors, including:[7]

- Acculturation attitude
- Migration status including reasons for migrating
- Personality and cognitive factors, such as self-esteem
- Other personal variables, such as gender and age
- Cultural distance and differences between the host culture and the person's culture of origin
- External factors, such as the attitudes and responses to migrants in the new society.

High levels of acculturative stress are associated with high levels of depression and increased levels of anxiety. The process of acculturation is rarely straightforward or short-lived. In fact, the effects of the migration

---

[7] www.mhima.org.au

experience can be long term and enduring. Effects may even be felt across lifetimes and generations. Increased levels of depression and anxiety are seen in second and third generation individuals with acculturative stress.

Unemployment and underemployment impact on a person's sense of self-worth and creates greater economic hardship, which contributes to an increased risk of mental ill health. Stable and meaningful employment is a strong protective factor to that and language acquisition plays a key role.

People with high levels of local language are

- likely to experience greater levels of employment
- more likely to experience fair employment conditions
- more easily able to access formal and informal supports
- able to reduce their risk of social isolation
- able to earn more respect, belonging and money

Refugees and asylum seekers are the most vulnerable people but they are also often highly resilient having survived terrible experiences.

The refugee experience can include witnessing or experiencing violence, abuse, imprisonment and torture. Refugees often face hazardous journeys, life in refugee camps and loss of, or separation from, family members. These traumatic experiences can have an impact on their mental health and well-being and may put them at increased risk of developing post-traumatic stress disorder (PTSD).

What is a Mental Health Condition?

Mental health conditions influence not only how someone feels (e.g., sad, frightened, worried, angry) but also how the person thinks, behaves and interacts with other people. There are several types, but the main groups are:

Mood Dsorders:

- depression (persistent sad mood, unmotivated, low energy, unable to find enjoyment)
- bipolar disorder (when depression symptoms alternate with extreme "highs"— elated, buzzing with activity and ideas, over-confident to an extreme).

Anxiety Disorders:

•   social anxiety (being terrified by what other people might think)

•   panic disorder (bursts of extreme anxiety with a range of physical symptoms)

•   agoraphobia (avoidance of situations and places that evoke fear of a panic attack)

•   obsessive-compulsive disorder (excessive checking, washing, or other rituals)

•   post-traumatic   stress   disorder (psychological distress following a traumatising event)

•   generalised anxiety (excessive worry about many aspects of life).

Psychotic Disorders:

•   schizophrenia (which includes strange experiences and beliefs, such as hallucinations and delusions, as well as social withdrawal and "flat" emotions)

•   some depression or bipolar disorders (when people also have hallucinations or delusions associated with their lows or highs).

Migrants who have been through a traumatic event, or witnessed someone else experience trauma have an increased risk of depression. If you have been through something traumatic, remember that once depression is diagnosed it can be treated; you can make a full recovery and go on living a happy and healthy life.

Typical symptoms of depression include:

- tiredness, lack of energy and motivation
- feeling worried or tense
- feeling bad, worthless or guilty
- having dark and gloomy thoughts, including thoughts of death or suicide
- feelings of unhappiness, moodiness and irritability, and sometimes emptiness or numbness
- losing interest and pleasure in activities that you once enjoyed
- loss of appetite and weight (but sometimes people "comfort eat" and put on weight)
- trouble sleeping, or over-sleeping and staying in bed most of the day.

Some common symptoms of anxiety:

- hot and cold flushes
- racing heart
- tightening of the chest

- snowballing worries
- obsessive thinking and compulsive behavior.

Personality disorders are slightly different—they describe maladaptive patterns of thinking, feeling and behaving that characterize the person across situations. Personality is regarded as being on a continuum from "normal" to "abnormal or disordered." Increasingly, diagnostic systems now recognise "maladaptive traits" or personality-based difficulties that fall between normal and abnormal personality. The presence of these personality factors can complicate other mental health conditions such as anxiety and depression, and interfere with social and occupational functioning. Substance abuse is a related issue that can have a devastating impact on the person's ability to function at work and to relate to their friends and family.

It is sad that there are some myths going on about this problem, such as:

- People with mental health conditions cannot work.
- Once people develop mental ill health, they will never recover.

- People with mental health conditions are dangerous.
- There's nothing I can do to help someone with a mental health condition.
- Mental ill health is a form of weakness.

Some facts about Mental Health around the world from WHO:

- Around 20% of the world's population are suffering from it. About half of mental disorders begin before the age of 14. Neuropsychiatric disorders are among the leading causes of worldwide disability in young people.

- Mental and substance use disorders are the leading cause of disability worldwide. About 23% of all years lost because of disability is caused by mental and substance use disorders.

- About 800,000 people commit suicide every year. Suicide is the second leading cause of death in 15-29-year-olds. There are indications that for each adult who died of suicide there may have been more than 20 others attempting suicide. 75% of suicides occur in low- and middle-income countries.

- Mental disorders are important risk factors for other diseases, as well as unintentional and intentional injury, HIV, cardiovascular disease and diabetes.

- Stigma and discrimination against patients and families prevent people from seeking mental health care.

- This stigma can lead to abuse, rejection and isolation and exclude people from health care or support.

- Shortages of psychiatrists, psychiatric nurses, psychologists and social workers are among the main barriers to providing treatment and care in low- and middle-income countries. But education and awareness towards mental illness also are instigators.

Not all mental illness is happening because of migration but as seen here, this problem is prevalent in the mobile world, and this would definitely include a lot of migrants in that bracket. Living in known environments people are vulnerable to this illness so with migration it can be bigger—no argument about that. Migrants please don't take these problems lightly. Please seek help. Talk to the right person. If not at least be open to the people in your close proximity. I have learnt through knowledge, patience and discipline that this phase can be treated if you are having difficulty, and to never be afraid to ask for help. There is absolutely no shame in doing so.

If you feel someone is going through symptoms, ask them at an appropriate, private moment about their feelings. It might be hard for them to talk, so try not to rush or be afraid.

Support the sufferer by helping them think through their options for feeling better. You might suggest they see a doctor or call a support service. Follow up after the conversation and keep doing things you enjoy together. It's the small things you do in supporting a friend that can make a big difference. Your friend may not want to talk about it yet, but at least they know you care and are willing to have the conversation when they're ready.

Give the person opportunities to talk. It can be helpful to let the person choose when to open up. Speak openly and honestly about your concerns. Let the person know you are concerned about them and are willing to help. Respect how the person interprets their symptoms. If the person doesn't feel comfortable talking to you, encourage them to discuss how they are feeling with someone else.

Treat the person with respect and dignity. Do not blame the person for their illness. Offer consistent emotional support and understanding. Encourage the person to talk. Give the person hope for recovery. Don't be sarcastic, nagging and over-involved or over-protective. Don't belittle or dismiss the person's feelings by saying things that may hurt. Try to cure the person or come up with answers to their problems.

CHAPTER 5

Different Society - Different Belief

"Society does not consist of individuals but expresses the sum of interrelations, the relations within which these individuals stand."
Karl Marx

As human beings, we all have our own values and beliefs which we have developed throughout the course of our lives. Our family, friends, community and the experiences we have had all contribute to our sense of who we are and how we view the world. When we migrate we end up in a different cultural set up and it is very important to be aware of our own personal values and beliefs and most importantly we should also be prepared to adopt or accept other views.

What are Values?

Values are principles, standards or qualities that an individual or group of people hold in high regard. These values guide the way we live our lives and the decisions we make. A value may be defined as something that we hold dear, those things / qualities which we consider to be of worth. Values always influence many of the judgments we make. Our values come from a variety of sources. These values can be identified with our race, gender, religion, language, culture and so on. Some of these include:

- family
- peers (social influences)
- the workplace (work ethics, job roles)
- educational institutions such as same schools or university
- significant life events (death, divorce, losing jobs, major accident and trauma, major health issues, significant financial losses)

- religion
- activities
- major historical events (wars, economic depressions, famine outbreak).

What is a Belief?

Beliefs come from real experiences. Our beliefs affect the quality of our work and all our relationships because what you believe is what you experience. We tend to think that our beliefs are based on reality, but it is our beliefs that govern our experiences. The beliefs that we hold are an important part of our identity. They may be religious, cultural or moral. Beliefs are precious because they reflect who we are and how we live our lives.

Multicultural Communication

So in this multicultural environment one major issue comes down to communication. Because again how we behave or communicate is how we feel inside. These things can be very sensitive and can even blow out of proportion. But if you take the positive side of it, interacting with other cultures can be very interesting. A cultural frame of reference is the way people from the same cultural group see their world; it is their world view. To effectively contribute in such scenarios be non-judgemental and respect others in their practices, show consideration, be polite, show genuine interest, respect privacy and confidentiality.

Initially just after migration when you are not fully familiar with social norms just be cooperative, you are in a seeking and exploring mode anyway. Listening to others, showing verbal and non-verbal respect and consideration, acknowledging your understanding of what others have said is always the best approach.

Working or living in isolation, being unwilling to listen to others, being unwilling to accept others' values and beliefs can act against you. You choose to migrate to this new land to solve some of your problems so be respectful of it. As we know "what goes around…comes around."

In this age of movement and multi-culture where people are mixing more than ever before everyone from community to corporates is talking about diversity—differences in seeing the world. Diversity depends on the following aspects:

- Race
- Colour
- Gender
- Sexual preference
- Age
- Physical or mental disability
- Marital status
- Family or carer's responsibilities
- Religion
- Political opinion
- National extraction
- Social origin

Diversity is a buzz word now. And culture means nothing but human behavior in context to their environment, values and so on. I was very keen to understand the game so that in my own way I can act more efficiently and consciously leading to more meaningful relationships for my surroundings and my organization.

Cultural Dimensions

Geert Hofstede is the stalwart in understanding and explaining cultural dimensions theory, a framework for cross-cultural communication. The theory was one of the first quantifiable theories that could be used to explain observed differences between cultures. This initial analysis identified systematic differences in national cultures on four primary dimensions:

- Individualism-Collectivism
- Power Distance
- Uncertainty Avoidance
- Masculinity-Femininity

These dimensions regard "four problem areas" that different societies handle differently. Later Professor Harry C. Triandis did extensive research and provided a useful tool to understand this cross-culture understanding predominantly focusing on the individualism(I)-collectivism(C) aspect.

To start with roughly 20% of the world's population (mainly in the western world) is individualistic, the rest would be (relatively) collectivistic. As countries become more affluent, their populations become more individualist. Cities are more individualistic than rural areas. Since human history, **the more scarce the resources, the more we prefer to be in a group or behave collectively**. It's the same thing.

Factors good to know:

- Adults tend to become more collectivist as they age.
- The affluent are more individualist than the poor.
- Women have more collectivist tendencies than men.
- Those whose occupations emphasize team work generally are more collectivist in their working environments than those whose occupations emphasize individual initiative and accomplishment.
- Education, travel and living abroad tend to expose people to diverse ideas, thereby increasing their individualism.
- Every country contains both individualists and collectivists, but most countries have a preponderance of one cultural type or the other purely based on resources.
- Individualists tend to view conflict as a natural part of human interaction.
- Collectivists, on the other hand, tend to view conflict as an irregularity.
- Individualists see dispute as an exciting and inspiring experience or as a root of personal and social change. Or on the other side, they see it as shameful inability to maintain harmonious relationships with others.

- Given their view of conflict as a natural phenomenon, individualists generally are able to acknowledge conflict and participate in a mediation without experiencing shame. For collectivists, however, even a tacit acknowledgement of conflict could cause a loss of face, and participation in a typical mediation might be an unwelcome experience.

- Collectivists might refuse to participate in voluntary mediation, and if mandatory, might resist orders to mediate. If mediation is unavoidable, they might exhibit signs of anxiety and confusion during the process.

- Individualists tend to prefer professional mediators who have specialized training in mediation procedures. For collectivists, there tends to be less of a concern about professional credentials and impartiality, but more of a concern that the mediator be an insider; someone who knows the parties or at least the context of their dispute.

- Individualists tend to view the parties to a dispute as those who are directly involved in it. Collectivists want a respected member should participate in a mediation session.

- Individualists prefer direct communication for conflict resolution whereas collectivists prefer conflict avoidance strategies.

Collectivist vs Individualist Culture Behavior:

- Those raised in a collectivist culture who then lived in an individualist culture for several years (migrants from developing to developed world) were high in both cultures. Those high in both are better adjusted and could deal with adversities more successfully.

- In C cultures the emphasis is on context more than content, they pay more attention to how something is said (tone of voice, gestures) than to what is said. Whereas in I cultures it is the opposite.

- C societies deal more with external factors such as norms, roles and values. But in I societies they focus on internal factors such as attitudes and personality.

- In C cultures people give priority to in-group goals rather than to personal goals. They see interpersonal relationships as one of the major parameters but in I cultures it is the other way round.

- I culture is high in expressiveness, dominance, initiation of action, aggressiveness, logical arguments, regulation of flow of communication and eye contact. They tend to finish the task and have strong opinions. C culture is high oi accommodating and avoidance of argument.

- People in C cultures use insulting words or swear to their families (mother $%^&er, sister $%^&er). In I cultures it is directed to that individual ($%^& you, *&^%head).

A study also found Individualistic culture increases when the person has been greatly exposed to the Western mass media. This also increases with affluence, when the person has a leadership role, education, has traveled internationally and has been socially mobile.

- I culture mothers portray the child as the protagonist in the talk, and to emphasize the child's and others' feelings and thoughts, whereas C culture mothers focused on norms, social roles, and emphasized behavioural expectations.

- In I culture, children are encouraged to talk more about their experiences and talk more about themselves.

- I culture kids are more specific and descriptive about specific events. Their memories tend to be expressive, detailed and lengthy. In contrast in C culture memories were found to be general, skeletal, less emotional, more neutral in their expression, and focused on routine events, on collective activities, on social interactions, on others or relations with others.

Nothing right or wrong it's just different. The more understanding you have more understanding and control you have if any conflict arise.

How They View the Issue

Personal preferences, needs, rights and goals are individualists' primary concerns, and they tend to place a high value on personal freedom and achievement. Self-reliance and competitiveness are common individualist traits. When personal goals conflict with group goals, individualists tend to give priority to their personal goals.

On the other hand, collectivists place the highest value on the interests of the group. Collectivists view themselves as interdependent and closely linked to one or more groups. They often are willing to maintain a commitment to a group even when their obligations to the group are personally disadvantageous. Norms, obligations and duties to groups are collectivists' primary concerns, and they tend to place a high value on group harmony and solidarity. Respectfulness and cooperation are common collectivist traits.

Factors Affecting Behavior

In individualist societies, however, children often are encouraged to identify personal preferences and to pursue personal goals and achievements. As a consequence, they begin to establish separate identities from their parents and other caregivers. The pursuit of personal goals that conflict with family norms may be acceptable, even expected. Children's successful cultivation of separate identities leads to a degree of detachment from their families by the time they are adults.

In contrast, when children of collectivist societies exhibit individualist tendencies, those tendencies frequently are discouraged. Compliance with group expectations and norms is praised. As a consequence, many children of collectivist societies learn to conform and to identify closely with their in-groups. As adults, they have strongly interdependent relationships with their families and other in-groups.

Individualists and collectivists hold dramatically different views of themselves and their proper relationships to others. As a consequence, their approaches to a problem and its resolution tend to diverge in equally dramatic ways. People more aware of these cultural norms become more effective communicators and mediators. At the end of the day, in this new land all these unknown acquaintances different culturally oriented people become your acquaintances, friends and families. So for effective adaptation and understanding, simply investigate information on others' behavior.

CHAPTER 6

Living in Mixed Culture

"The range of what we think and do is limited by what we fail to notice. And because we fail to notice we fail to change until we notice how failing to notice shapes our thoughts and deeds."
Daniel Goleman

I believe you must learn to make the best use of whatever resources you have at your disposal and you must be ready to learn important skills that you might not have. It is only by learning to make the best use of your life that you can live your own dreams.

You must always believe that life is a journey, not a destination. There are lots of people in this world who either do as they were told since childhood or for financial viability. Putting yourself in survival mode is important but devoting your life to it makes no sense at all. By doing this, one keeps getting further away from exposure to certain sectors of life in which they might excel. For example, a person may dance effortlessly well, but is hidden away working in the banking industry. I know this is normal but we who can't pursue such paths do so predominantly because of fear.

It has been said that FEAR is False Evidence Appearing Real, but in this uncertainty it mainly comes in three ways:

1. from our past experiences
2. from our future anticipations
3. from peer pressure and social norms which are sometimes difficult to follow

The first two points are quiet understandable but I personally feel fear from peer pressure or social norms is the most devastating and disrespecting experience that someone can have. This is very true for all migrants because in initial settlement they can't and don't choose acquaintances, it just happens to them. And after that, many of them keep following these acquaintances from fear of being lonely or isolated. Your consciousness as an individual and the collective sum of the consciousness of the people you are with combined give you a weighted impact on who you become.

Sociologist Robert Nisbet says society as a whole may encourage or discourage the development of individual characteristics. A genius can grow in a social group more easily if the intellectual atmosphere of the group nurtures geniuses. But we also protect our social setting to provide experiences that foster the growth of genius in our society. This pretty much boils down to people with whom you are spending time. I really like this quote by Jim Rohn: "You are the average of the five people you spend the most time with."

Things to Remember in Migration

1. You should strongly believe that you migrate to solve some of the problems that are a source of stress in your home land.
2. You must remember you migrated to chase your dream.

3. Understand each phase of migration and identify where you are from your behavior.
4. As a migrant you must take pride in your risk-taking abilities.
5. After initial settlement keep reminding yourself the reason and zeal for migration.
6. Absorb or understand as much of the new culture as possible, as the more you know about the culture the better one can adjust.
7. Like your first day of migration keep that seeking, open mindset to learn new things.
8. Be polite, respectful to others' culture, identity and behavior. Focus on personal branding and making it very rich in all senses.
9. A mind-set that "nothing is perfect, it's just different" gives you openness towards different perspectives. It helps you build and maintain true relationships, surrounded by people who uplift you, enhance you and motivate you in your down time.
10. Don't get sucked into the environment immediately available to you. Keep yourself motivated and joyful, find courage to get out of your comfort zone again and again as you did in the past.

It has been proven that migrants who usually end up being unsuccessful are those who display the following attributes in their behavior:

- always compare the life they left behind
- after initial settlement, refuse to bear hardships and search for comfort alone
- only after material comforts; cars, houses etc. and refuse to explore their true selves believing it is too risky due to the changed environment they are exposed to
- always search for their own community and stick strongly to the traditional beliefs and norms
- live life with a low sense of purpose and low self-esteem, and always find ways not to open themselves to exploring new things
- are susceptible to adapt to new land, creating lots of stress and building an attitude of saying "no" and complaining
- finding faults about everything in the new culture, negative mindset which leads to self-sabotaging and demoralising relationships
- can't form and maintain meaningful relationships with outer community
- are ungrateful and lack of integrity, depend on some resourceful individual in times of need and don't return the favour

- live daunted by peer pressure, unable to find their true selves, just go with the flow and survival mindset all the time

By now you should have understood that the whole journey towards effective migration is yours and only yours. You should not get bogged down by external problems; you should instead evolve as a human being from these problems, find your true self within and work towards the achievement of your true self.

In the modern world a frequently used word is "deadline." Keep in mind that deadlines can only be incorporated to a task which has been done before, which has been created by someone before you and you are just doing it in your own way. In your own life there may be a deadline for an interview, changing jobs etc. but no deadline for the person you want to become. There can be no deadline for knowledge. It's all about trying to work harder and to build the right attitudes. Keep focus on what you want to be and keep working towards it. Just enjoy the journey and do things which give you happiness because if you keep yourself happy, you can keep others happy. It is only by doing something really meaningful, enhancing your personality that will give you a true sense of achievement, adding value to your journey.

Raising a Child in a Different Culture

Many migrants face problems raising their children in the new land due to lack of family support, cultural inadaptability, financial inadequacy and lack of social support. But to raise them successfully cultural competency is a crucial thing. And it is a life long journey, not a destination. Encourage children to be aware of their own world view, develop positive attitudes towards cultural differences, help them to gain knowledge of different cultural practices and world views and develop skills for communication and interaction across cultures. Children need to be taught to respect, appreciate and positively interact with people who are different from them.

Parenting young children while migrating to another land can be very hard. Parents must deal with caring for children and the children's experience of migration, as well as their own difficulties and experiences. These experiences can be both physical and emotional and can include:

- dealing with language difficulties and feeling isolated because it's hard to communicate
- experiencing grief and a sense of loss from being separated from family, friends, culture and identity within a familiar community
- feeling frustrated at not being able to find employment or a job to use qualifications or skills
- finding it difficult to find assistance, support and services in the new community
- struggling to cope financially
- feeling lonely, hopeless or overwhelmed at such an enormous life change, to the point where it becomes too much and they develop a mental illness
- feeling alone because they don't feel like part of the community or feel they don't belong.

Young children don't have much say in whether they migrate—it's usually a decision made by their parents. In some instances, the experience can be very unsettling as children adjust to their new life and deal with the loss of the old home while missing friends, familiar sights, sounds and smells. The most important factor for children's emotional well-being during this period is having a stable home environment while the family adjusts to the change.

Children's experience of migration also depends on their age. Younger children and babies might not understand what's going on. But because they're completely dependent on their parents, their emotional experience will reflect their parents' experience in many ways. Toddlers busy testing out their independence, need parents to provide a secure environment for exploration. If parents are anxious or there's major disruption, children might have behavior problems.

Older children's experience of migration also depends on their sense of self and how secure they feel in their new environment. Adjusting to a new school and meeting new friends can play a big role in children's ability to deal with migration. Many children cope very well, many don't. As children become older, they often play a central role in the whole family's experience of migration. Children often pick up language skills faster than adults and in some instances parents rely on children to communicate for them; this responsibility may put too much pressure on the children.

Expectations from Parents

Parents have behavioral expectations of their children that are similar in many cultures. Normally children should be respectful and polite, not interrupt, be honest, share and do well in school. However, some cultures have additional expectations. According to the Centres for Disease Control and Prevention, Asian and Caucasian parents expect children to exert self-control, while African, African-American, Latino and American Indian fathers often feel their children should have a religious or spiritual foundation.

According to a National Foster & Kinship Care Conference report, West African, Arabic and Asia-Pacific communities often stop practices such as kissing or hugging a child once it becomes a toddler. However, some cultures consider physical attention such as bathing, skin care or braiding a child's hair to be appropriate physical ways to express affection. Monetary rewards and praise are also signs of affection in these cultures. Many parents see educational attainment as desirable for their children. In some Chinese families, however, physical punishment might be used to induce children to study hard and get good grades.

Furthermore, Asian and Indian families might also exert considerable pressure on their child to achieve scholastically.

As the world is getting smaller and smaller we should raise our next generation who are well adaptive with the fast changing world. In today's interconnected global world, one of the greatest gifts we can give our children is to prepare them to thrive in the new world marketplace. We must inspire our children to be curious about the world and to become globally aware. We must teach our children to appreciate, communicate and interact with people across different cultures and in other countries and encourage the development of soft skills critical to cross-cultural competence. Curiosity and the ability to question things, ability to carefully listen and observe, flexibility and creativity should be the way to go as well as providing a solid grounding in your home culture. In order for children to be comfortable in the world, they must feel comfortable at home. Constant learning, exploring different things should be encouraged. The more open and knowledgeable they are about the surroundings, the more fearless and ambitious they will become. And when they are on their own step back, relax and enjoy the show.

It is widely known that diversity has the potential to bring many benefits in human life. However, it is difficult to access these benefits when differences clash and emotions take center stage. Often individuals, even intelligent ones, do not know how to deal with these feelings to capitalize on diverse perspectives, styles and approaches. Developing the capacity to understand and manage feelings and deal effectively with others, no matter how great the differences are, is a critical competence in today's diverse society. The ability to do so depends in great part on emotional intelligence. You, as a migrant, may come face to face with three significant career de-railers in your journey towards achievement: difficulty in handling change, inability to work in a diverse team and poor interpersonal relations.

What is Emotional Intelligence in Diversity?

While human beings function on both rational and emotional levels, emotions are at the heart of our energy, commitment and motivation. Feelings are also fundamental in forming our reactions to the differences we see in others, whether we approach or avoid, like or dislike, accept or reject. The more we understand and manage our emotional responses, the more we enjoy greater comfort in relationships, effectiveness in interactions and peace within ourselves. So as a migrant you have to be careful and keep a close eye on the ability to feel, understand, articulate, manage and apply the power of emotions to interactions across lines of difference. [8]

According to the authors of "Emotional Intelligence and Diversity (EID)" the key points to remember to achieve your optimum integration for individuals and organizations working with diverse force are:

Affirmative Introspection: requires self-awareness combined with self-reflection on the individual's values, passions, preferences, and worldview.

- Be comfortable in your own skin
- Be in tune with your own biases and hot buttons
- Be honest with yourself about your reactions, feelings and values

---

[8], "Emotional Intelligence and Diversity" Lee Gardenswartz, Jorge Cherbosque and Anita Rowe

- When you have a strong reaction to a situation or another's behavior, ask yourself why
- Be willing to comment on in a non-judgmental and objective way

Self-Governance: means managing emotional reactions to differences among people and to specific situations, so that the behavioral responses the individual chooses create constructive effect rather than self-defeating and destructive results.

- Develop ways to help yourself cope with ambiguity and be your own change master
- Be aware of new and unfamiliar environments, avoid finger pointing and blaming
- Seek and be open, welcome other opinions while managing rather than becoming defensive
- Manage frustration and anger by reframing situations and changing self-talk messages
- Encourage fun ways to enhance the enjoyment of surroundings and alleviate stress

Intercultural Literacy: refers to continually and nonjudgmentally exploring and understanding others' cultural norms in terms of values, beliefs, and behaviors.

- Understand cultural whys behind behaviour and respect, understand and value differences, identify and maintain trust and integrity
- See the benefits and limitations of all norms
- Assume that difficult behavior takes place for a reason and find out what the reason is
- Reach out to those who are different to expand your understanding
- Avoid negative attributions and invest time in understanding others' behaviors as a way to improve relationships

Social Architecting: is a deliberate and conscious effort to structure relationships and social environments to increase the likelihood of productive and mutually beneficial relationships.

- Serving as a cultural interpreter
- Communicating effectively and resolving conflicts in diverse settings
- Structure synergistic environments, seek resolutions that are mutually satisfying
- Spending time building relationships with people different from you

- Expressing gratitude to others on a regular basis

Exact acceptance of reality need not be synonymous with capitulation, humiliating defeat. Acceptance is about using the lessons we learned in life to come to terms with the realities of the world, on our own terms. In a migrant's life there are lots of ups and downs as the quicker we accept the situation the better we will be able to act in our own lives.

CHAPTER 7

Pursuit of Happiness

The pursuit of happiness is a fundamental human right, but what exactly is happiness? Why do some people always seem to be happy and some are never happy? From a holistic point of view, what is well-being?

Scientists, psychologists, doctors and gurus all agree that people who live with more happiness or well-being have better social and work relationships; make more money; live longer, healthier lives; and are more contributory societal citizens.

Well-being is not just the absence of disease or

illness. It is a complex combination of a person's physical, mental, emotional and social health factors. Well-being is strongly linked to happiness and life satisfaction. In short, well-being could be described as how you feel about yourself and your life.

Every aspect of your life influences your state of well-being. Many people—especially economic migrants—believe that wealth is a fast track to happiness. Yet various international studies have shown that it is the quality of our personal relationships, not the size of our bank balances, which has the greatest effect on our state of well-being.

Money is linked to well-being because having enough money improves living conditions and increases social status. Believing that money is the key to happiness can also harm a person's well-being. Research shows that people who pursue "extrinsic" goals such as money and fame are more anxious, depressed and dissatisfied than people who value "intrinsic" goals like close relationships with loved ones. It has been proven that a person's well-being depends on happy intimate relationships, enough money, an enjoyable and fulfilling career, regular exercise, proper diet, sleep, spiritual or religious beliefs, healthy self-esteem with an optimistic outlook and sense of purpose and belonging. As Simon Sinek rightly said, "Working hard for something we don't care about is called stress; working hard for something we love is called passion."

A recent Australian consumer study into well-being showed some interesting statistics: 58% of adults and 79% of parents with children less than 18 years old, wish to spend more time on improving their well-being. A staggering 83% are prepared to pay more money for products or services that enhance their feelings of well-being.

There is a lot of research conducted in Western countries about this yet the results may not be reliably generalized to all countries and cultures. I will try to give some perspectives from both Eastern and Western worlds . When it comes to Western or individualist societies the factors are predominantly extrinsic in nature; personality, living standards, activities and cultural factors are significant.

Western Influence

Research gives a fairly unambiguous picture that for those of us who live in rich countries, psychological factors, especially our personality, are by far the most important factor in how happy we are. Our personality affects how we think, feel and act. Highly beneficial for positive emotions are emotional stability, an open mind and extroverted behavior. Emotionally stable people are rarely worried; they are optimistic and recover quickly from negative experiences. Extroverted people are more active in their spare time and have a characteristically high rate of interaction with friends and colleagues. All these features have been shown to have a strong positive effect on both life satisfaction and well-being. The character trait of emotional stability can make a person react more routinely and less negatively affected by setbacks, bad experiences and the general adversities of life. Intelligence or rhetorical talents have no influence on this.

The market culture or the "rich and beautiful" concept teaches us that money is the source of well-being. It is altogether too often accepted that more income is equivalent to more happiness. A relatively recent study by E.

Diener and S. Oishi shows that income is only weakly linked to subjective satisfaction. Even being at the very top of the income-pyramid does not necessarily mean having a more positive attitude towards life, as a study by the London School of Economics indicates. It showed that the rate of depression and suicidal tendencies among the high-earners is higher than in other parts of society.

The standard of living affects the variation between people's happiness by only 10%-15%. Maslow's need-hierarchy theory is relevant in these cases—other needs, for example self-fulfilment, become more prominent when material and social needs are fulfilled.

Social relations play an important role in our well-being. In a study of very happy people, researchers Seligman and Diener found that good social relations were the most important thing to them. Our well-being increases when we spend time with people we like. Loving and meaningful relations are very important.

People who are active during their spare time tend to be happier than people who spend their free time passively. People who get involved in charity are happier than average; people who spend a lot of time watching television or spend time on social media tend to be less happy. Confessions of faith and membership in a religious community are often accompanied with optimistic feelings, social activities and a decrease in stress.

Psychographic Factors and Meaning of Life

The famous psychiatrist Viktor E. Frankl, examined the human search for meaning and called it "Self-Transcendence." This term serves as a description of a positive result in the individual search for meaning together with long-term emotions of happiness. His model—similar to Maslow's idea—is all about self-fulfilment and personal goal setting in life, so that one creates his own meaning of life which includes ethical norms and benchmarks for the whole process and way of living. Personal aims in life define a proper and meaningful way of life and provide people with opportunities for life planning and structuring. Our hopes, wishes and thoughts then follow these goal settings and create a bigger picture. A life completely without goals is one without meaning and therefore negative emotions like senselessness might occur more often. A good society is a well-developed inclusion of migrants, good infrastructure and administration, which are all related to positive effects of improvements for a better life satisfaction.

Eastern Philosophy

"We become victims of mental illness because of pent up envy, jealousy, anger, pride, super ego, hatred and hostility. Our health takes a toll owing to negative thoughts. The secret of good health is purity of thoughts," said Professor B. M. Hegde. "One becomes mentally ill because he is unnecessarily concerned about others. If one has his mind under control, he will have good health." He strongly says, "Mind your mind to stay healthy." It is more of "Mind over Body" which has to be taken care of for ensuring our well-being—keep away from these negative thoughts.

In last 100 years science and technology have been brought comfort and convenience our way; never before could any other generation even dream of these kinds of superiority. Human beings are not well because though we have taken care of the outside, we never bothered to take care of the inside. Stress does not come from the nature of our work; stress is our inability to manage our own system. Only when there are no inner confusions and dilemma, can we handle the outside issues well. So if we truly want to enhance the quality of our life, we have to take step and be willing to invest a little bit of time for our inner well-being.

According to Sadhguru "Real human well-being will happen only when a man is peaceful and joyful within himself. Only when we are peaceful and joyful by our own nature, will we pursue life without any fear or anxiety. As long as there is a fear—What will happen to me?—within us, we will only take half strides in life; we will never take full strides. So if a human being wants to find his full potential, the first thing is, there should be an inner stability. No matter who we are or how powerful we are, outside situations are not always going to be 100 per cent in our control. This is because the outside situation involves a million different ingredients. We just hope that it will all fall into place."

Everything in this universe—the air we breathe, the water we drink, the food we eat, the surroundings in which we live, the society and the culture thereof, our friends, our family, our job, our colleagues, the atmospheric temperature of the place where we live, the planets in the cosmos, our religious beliefs, the monetary economy that we practice and, above all, our all-pervading consciousness, which is a tiny part of the universal consciousness—matters at the end of the day, to keep us healthy.

Your happiness and well-being is in your hands. A happy mind helps to keep the body healthy. A healthy body is the result of a happy mind that follows altruism as its motto. Disease is an accident. In conclusion, you can live with the fullest well-being, if you mind your mind to remain healthy.

With migration you have already put yourself in a position which tested your risk-taking ability. Do it again and again. Don't stop; don't settle. Keep learning and keep your mind open. I strongly believe if you are a migrant you are already ahead and half way to success, well-being and happiness.

CHAPTER 8

Our New Future

"The illiterate of the 21st century will not be those who cannot read and write, but those who cannot learn, unlearn, and relearn."
Alvin Toffler

We need to be futuristic and optimistic to understand the best in our future generations. Because of time, technology, information and many other factors these generations behave in certain ways which many find funny— irrelevant to older generations—but the truth is they will shape the new world and our future as a whole. Let's have a look at the different generations.

Baby Boomers who are aged roughly 47-65 and nearly approaching retirement age, the "boomers" are those born in the decade following the end of World War II. They are considered a generation who have "had it all," sheltered by parents. Many benefited from free tertiary education and relatively low housing costs. Common put-downs range from: self-obsessed" to "stuck in their ways."

Generation X: They were born roughly between 1963 and1980 (now aged early-30s to mid-40s.) Gen-Xers are often labelled the "slacker" generation, uncommitted and unfocused—the "why me?" generation. They are the first generation to have experienced divorce on a large scale and are likely to have changed careers several times. Their parents grew up in mostly collective society and lived in close proximity with each other. They mostly find comfort while raising children but not necessarily in their own journey and are more considered to keep their heads down than to change the world.

Generation Y: They were born between 1981 and 1994. Common put-downs include lazy, debt-ridden and programmed for instant gratification. They are portrayed as demanding and unrealistic in their career aspirations. Now we can add "internet-addicted" and "lonely" to the list. But they are also the most adaptable, creative generation in history. Today 80 million millennials are in the workforce. Technological changes and globalization now will forever change how we live and work. Millennials believe job security is a thing of the past, and the education system isn't delivering in the way that it should. With so much unpredictability, this generation has learned to adapt and iterate in ways their parents never could have imagined—even if they are living in their parents' basements. As this generation is now big time in the work force, I will focus on that.

Generation Z: They were born between 1995 and 2009 and are the first generation never to have experienced the pre-internet world. Some call them the "iPad generation." Then comes **Generation Alpha**—it has been predicted they will be the most formally educated generation in history, beginning school earlier and studying longer.

The reason I am talking about millennials or Generation Y is because by 2020:

- **they will form 50% of the global workforce**
- **59% of them would be willing to move to a foreign country for a job**

Millennials strongly believe they can change the world. They hate the status-quo and are utter non-believers in any hierarchy that may be social or professional. They are the most threatening and exciting generation in social revolution.

We talk about migrants and new comers but this coming generations will just look at it as a normal way of life. With this tremendous human movement in the coming decades the world will truly be a global village. All cultures and races will mix, we will have better understanding towards humanism and we will literally feel the whole world as a family rather than just an opportunistic market place.

I personally always find it fascinating to work with the young blood because of their fearless nature. Erica Dhawan wrote "Technology has convinced millennials that a single person's voice can make a difference." I always find inspiration from these budding generations and I believe it's good to send this message across because we have no other choice but to adapt with this changing demography of workforce. There is a lot of research done by different organisations on this topic.

- The millennial generation is the most educated generation in history.
- They probably live with maximum debt.
- They are ambitious. They expect to be in a management position in quick time.
- Loyalty to the organization is not particularly strong but they strongly believe business should be measured on its act towards improving society.
- They are not concerned about the title but more on integrity and giving back to society.
- They are the first global-centric generation, having come of age during the rapid growth of the Internet.
- They are among the most resilient in navigating change while deepening their appreciation for diversity and inclusion.
- They have the most number of single parents, yet the most positive attitude toward marriage and children.
- They prefer to work with businesses doing ethical practices, social impact and prosperity to mankind.
- They prefer to view their managers as friend, peer, coach, or mentor. They strongly admire those with experience or knowledge over position or power.

The internet, technology and social media have turned this generation into having an instant fix mentality. A recent study suggests, six out of 10 millennials would rather spend money on experiences than material things. Nearly half of them share experiences through social media. Instead of saving money for a new purse, laptop, or car many young people are hoarding their money to spend it instead on festival experiences around the world. They are Social Travelers.

What I really like most is millennials are creating a change in how work gets done, as they work more in teams and use more technology. Leigh Buchanon writes in *Meet the Millennials*, "One of the characteristics of millennials, besides the fact that they are masters of digital communication, is that they are primed to do well by doing good. Almost 70 percent say that giving back and being civically engaged are their highest priorities."

The Millennial Influence

A report by Deloitte titled "The millennial influence in the workplace" says millennials view diversity as the blending of different backgrounds, experiences, and perspectives within a team, which is known as cognitive diversity. They believe cognitive diversity works through engagement, empowerment, and authenticity.

They value open participation from individuals with different ideas and perspectives that have a positive impact on surroundings. Leadership should be transparent, communicative, and engaging. They also believe rather than the education or identities, their characteristics bring value to the business. They value community, family, and creativity in their work.

But according to the American Psychological Association's annual report, "Stress across generations," concerns about money and finances are the biggest cause of stress and millennials are most affected by that. While stress obviously has psychological manifestations like frustration and anxiety, so too the health effects of stress are a growing concern. Financial stress has been linked to high blood pressure and other general health problems—which is probably connected to the way mental health can affect physical health. Women, parents, and people with lower incomes are disproportionally affected by stress, reporting symptoms like inability to sleep, irritability, anxiety, lack of motivation, unhealthy behaviors, and not being able to make life changes that would help them better cope with stress.

Female Millennials

Organisations all over the world are currently facing the challenges that come with vast numbers of millennial talent entering and reshaping the workforce. In parallel, they are also challenged with a lack of women in leadership positions. A new era of talent reported by PricewaterhouseCoopers (PwC) mentions that females are becoming a larger part of the global talent pool.

- Female millennials are more career-confident and ambitious than their previous generations.
- Diversity is very much front of mind.
- A gender role model gap still exists but is eradicating because of awareness and socio economic changes.
- Work-life strategies and global careers are high on the agenda.

Global Work Force 2020

The world's work force will become even more mobile, and employers will increasingly reach across borders to find the skills they need. These movements of workers will be driven by the growing gap between the world's supplies of labor and the demand for it. There will be massive relocations of people, including migrants, temporary workers, retirees, and visitors. The greatest relocations will involve young, well-educated workers flocking to the cities of the developed world. Women will enter the work force in great numbers.

According to Josh Bersin, founder of Bersin & Associates (now Bersin by Deloitte), said we see five fundamental shifts which dramatically impact corporate talent, leadership, and HR strategies. Technology has removed the barrier between work and life. Companies have to focus on culture, environment and simplification. Employee engagement, culture, and leadership are lifeline issues. Learning, capabilities, and skills are the currency of success. Data is now integral to all decisions on human dynamics. Employees are "always on"—hyper connected to their jobs through pervasive mobile technology. Networking tools like LinkedIn, Facebook, and Glassdoor enable people to easily monitor the market for new job opportunities. Details about an organization's culture are available at the tap of a screen, providing insights about companies to employees and potential employees alike. The balance of power in the employer-employee relationship has shifted—making today's employees more like customers or partners than subordinates.

The utilization of the global workforce is very prevalent; people are moving both across borders and within a country. Economic prosperity, the rapid rise in educational standards in parts of the developing world, and greater integration across markets continue to contribute to labor mobility and cross-border migration. So scenarios are favouring migrants' acceptance from the host nation. It is migrants' responsibility now to take the most advantage.

The Future of Work

"The future of work – A journey to 2022", a report by PwC suggests some drastic stuff:

- 2016 - $10 tablet computer comes on to the market

- 2017 - Assembly workers in a factory in Hanoi start wearing sensors to gauge concentration, work rate and mood
- 2018 - Analysts attend presentation by Fortune 500 Chief Performance Officer, who heads a combined Finance and HR function
- 2019 - Doctor in China carries out "remote" surgery on patient in Ghana
- 2020 - Rioting sweeps across university campuses as students lose patience with lack of job opportunities
- 2021 - Licences granted for driverless cars
- 2022 - World's first fully automated and robot-served hotel opens

Tremendous forces are radically reshaping the world of work. Economic shifts are redistributing power, wealth, competition and opportunity around the globe. Disruptive innovations, radical thinking, new business models and resource scarcity are impacting every sector. Managing complexity as well as ambiguity will have the single biggest impact on the way we work over the next 10 years.[9] Most organisations are likely to be a mix of three worlds of work.

---

[9] http://www.pwc.com/managing-tomorrows-people/future-of-work/future-of-work-report-v23.pdf

The Orange World: Where small is beautiful, big is bad. Companies begin to break down into collaboration networks of smaller organisations; specialisation dominates the world economy. Businesses are fragmented and companies are small and nimble, relying on an extensive network of suppliers. Companies have multiple clients and contracts and they routinely supplement their workforce with a globally diverse network of "team workers"—technologically savvy, networked employees who are contracted on a supply and demand basis, anywhere in the world.

The Green World: Mid-size companies where social responsibility dominates the corporate agenda with concerns about changes in climate and demographics, and embedding sustainability are becoming the key drivers of business. Where companies have developed a powerful social conscience that's closely tied to their brand. Their focus is on sustainable and ethical business practice and they attract employees with values that reflect their own. Their success is largely driven by a high degree of employee engagement. This impacts business decisions about mobility and the way employees work.

The Blue World : Where corporate is king, big company capitalism rules as organizations continue to grow bigger and individual preferences override belief in collective social responsibility. These companies have invested heavily in the talent pipeline and believe in developing people as assets and take a paternal approach to their workforce. While the work is pressurized and fast-paced, employees are committed, well trained and more likely to remain with a single employer long-term.[10]

The World in 2020 and Beyond

Explosive growth in emerging markets is creating a huge increase in the number of employees working outside their home location and critical shortages in talent in specific markets and disciplines have pushed mobility up the boardroom agenda.

The growing importance of emerging markets has created a significant shift in mobility patterns. Skilled employees from emerging markets are increasingly in demand at home and abroad. Domestic multinationals are

---

[10] http://www.pwc.com/managing-tomorrows-people/future-of-work/pwc-talent-mobility-2020.pdf

increasingly attractive to local talent. Most millennials want and expect an overseas assignment during their career.

By 2020, governments and regulators will need to accept the economic benefits of talent mobility to stimulate economic growth. This acceptance smooths the way to greater collaboration between governments and businesses to remove some of the barriers to mobility around the world. Technology will play a key role in global working arrangements and help to support compliance obligations; however, technology will not erode the need to have people deployed "on the ground."

Urban populations will rise at a great rate, meaning intra-country migration will increase. The world urban population is expected to increase by 72% by 2050, from 3.6 billion in 2011 to 6.3 billion in 2050. Virtually all of the expected growth in the world population will be concentrated in the urban areas of the less developed regions. New cities' population shifts will have a strong influence on where organizations will do business over the coming decades. Much of the population growth over the next 30 years will be concentrated around urban areas in emerging economies as these countries begin to mirror developed economies.

Today, for example, in developed countries 75% of the population live in urban areas and this will rise to 84% by 2030; in less developed regions only 40% live in urban areas today, but this will increase to 56% by 2030. Housing, schools and hospitals soon follow and a new thriving city, ripe for multinationals will be a normal way of living. The emergence of new commercial centers away from capital cities will create a new demand for domestic mobility. Short-term assignments, often lasting a year or less have become more popular; 20% of assignments now last less than 12 months, compared with 10% in 2002. Short-term assignments are generally more appealing to younger workers who want to broaden their experience than to those with families, as disruption is minimized. Project-based assignments will be norm. Organizations are bringing selected employees from different parts of the organization together for a specific project, requiring some to relocate temporarily, or travel frequently while the work is carried out. Intra-country mobility is on the rise as organizations look to maximize their investment in mobility.

Regional leaders often find that their role requires extensive business travel and as a result they are constantly on the move. Similarly, some specialists move from project to project to the extent that they effectively have no "home" country. Organizations may move their regional or global headquarters in order to be closer to business interests and the fastest-growing markets, meaning the permanent relocation of key managers and their families.

Finally multiculturalism is more like a multiracial community with a broadly common culture and one language, (mainly English in western countries). Increasingly people are comfortable with a more fluid sense of identity. Nevertheless, it is our job to assimilate and have an established community, which serves as a link between old and new; not just a security blanket but a springboard to connecting with people from other backgrounds. We migrants have to have a sense of belonging and connection—because we chose this new land as our home by choice, not by accident.

CHAPTER 9

A Bouquet For You

"Societies, organizations, and individuals represent the gardens, bouquets and flowers of social science."
Geert Hofstede

Rose

Throughout human history, migration has been a courageous expression of the individual's will to overcome adversity and to live a better life. Time and time again it provides improvement of economic and social conditions at both origin and destination. To mark that the

International Organization for Migration (IOM) at the first global Candlelight Vigil on 18 December 2015 called for all the international community to come together and remember the refugees and migrants who have lost their lives or have disappeared while trying to reach a safe harbor after arduous journeys across seas and deserts as "International Migrants Day."

Roger Merchant – story of a dream to be someone with persuasion

Born in Goa Roger moved to London at the age of 7 with his two brothers and a sister. He stayed there 2 years with absolute hardship as his father couldn't find any way to survive and with huge debt and a broken heart, returned to Goa. Somehow he managed to finish school with very poor marks. He was very passionate about rugby and at 15 he became MC for his local church programmes. According to Roger they gave him the best sales and public speaking training. By 18 years of age he was earning reasonable money but migrated to Melbourne.

With no university degree and a family to support, he entered into a clerical job. Within 6 months he became bored and changed to a bank. With his go-getting attitude, after a couple of promotions he became branch manager within 2 years. He started playing rugby but without thinking what was next. Seeing an advertisement for a next generation computer course he felt computers could be the next big thing in business. He joined a 3 year course at the University of Melbourne in next generation computers. The fees were more than his annual salary but he took a loan to complete his education. As a driven person he became the head of IT as branches started implementing computers, and he was the only employee with a computer degree.

To get more of a challenge he left the bank and joined an IT company as a pre-sales and programming manager. He worked there for 3 years and in the last 2 years was the consistent top sales representative for that company globally, becoming National Sales Manager. In 1990 he was asked by a friend to join his business and build it up because he wanted to leave family and material life to become a priest. The enterprise had 6 staff initially. He took over as CEO and increased the business to a $35M turnover with 220 staff.

He is married to an Australian woman and they have 3 sons. He tells me that trust, integrity and a strong personal brand are the most precious things. Roger is one of the mentors in my life where I know our friendship is a shelter for me: it's a place where I can be fully vulnerable, weak and sad. And at the end of it I know I will come out stronger, more confident and more courageous.

Cherry Blossom

Trends in migration will change over the next couple of years; the number of refugees worldwide will rise to new historic levels; migrants will send home more money than ever before; there will be more women migrants than men and the global war for talent will intensify.

Preeti Sen – story about believing in yourself

"I was habituated to migratory behavior since childhood because my father was in government and got transferred to a new station every 3 years. I have lived in 7 different states within India. In 2005 I migrated to

Sydney to join my husband then in 2007 moved to Melbourne.

"In my teenage years, we used to make friends at one place and then it would be time to move to another place. I had lost my parents at a young age so that has brought lots of ups and downs during one phase. But at the same time it made me strong and more independent. Moving to an international city after marriage was a bit strange but not difficult because of my multicultural background. I was into sports, cultural and arts and I started that immediately after migration. I always liked adventure sports; I have done sky diving, bungee jumping and climbed the Sydney Harbor Bridge.

"I see every failure as a step towards success; I always try to be positive. I did a special welcome dance for Shivaji Ganeshan (a popular south Indian actor) for a south Indian community programme. The more exposure you get to the outside world, the more you evolve culturally, the more confident, independent and individual you become. I have always been positive about whatever life brings on for me. I like to socialize wherever I get a positive vibe and feel-good factor and there is something new to see or learn."

Sunflower

People who move to wealthier land surely expect that migration will lead them to a better life. In reality they often live in a lower economic status. In economic terms, what matters for happiness is the way one compares oneself to others. Even when income rises significantly, leading to upward mobility, people often adjust their reference groups, comparing themselves to others at a higher level rather than deriving satisfaction from comparing themselves to a stable reference group.

Rodney Smith – go back to Wimbledon

Rodney was born and brought up in England. He was very much into sports since childhood and played professional tennis and squash for several years. He was junior Wimbledon champion and played squash at county level. As a profession it was a small source of income and he was working as an employee but at the age of 30 he started his own consultancy business. It went very well then there was a tremendous loss of money and lots of debt. After that with his wife and 2 children migrated to Wellington, New Zealand.

After living with the British class culture that he didn't enjoy, New Zealand seemed welcoming. After 2 years he migrated to Australia with no job; that was the really tough part. Initially he didn't feel very welcome. As he was from New Zealand he felt strongly something of a "little brother" syndrome and people didn't recognize his ability and experience. Sport really helped me to mingle and socialize with locals.

He got a role in a national consultancy firm and worked for next 5 years and finally became the CIO of that firm. He was national coach for juniors in squash for 2 consecutive years. One day he resigned from a CIO role and started his consultancy business again and although it had its ups and downs, he is happy, free and has more control in his life.

Rodney says, "You don't always need a plan. Sometimes you just need to breathe, trust, let go and see what happens. Whenever I get stuck in life I go back to my Wimbledon days where I came from nowhere and conquered and that self-belief keeps me going all the time."

Lily

I personally like Li Ka Shing's wisdom—a billionaire and one of the richest men in Asia. He is a true example of someone who came from the gutter and made it to the top. This article first appeared in CeoConnectz. He said you should split your income into 5 separate funds, which should last you for the entire month.

1. The very first set of funds should be used to meet your living expenses.

2. The second set of funds will be used to network and meet new people—at least 2 new people every month who are smarter than you and ask tons of questions. Buy lunch for them who are more knowledgeable, richer than you or people who have helped you in your career.

3. The third set of funds is for learning purposes—buy books, attend seminars and courses.

4. The fourth set is more of an optional set that he recommends for travel. His belief is that everyone should travel at least once in a year and enjoy themselves. Use that experience to recharge yourself and gain

more motivation to do better.

5.   Your last set should be saved in your bank.

Things to Do When You are Poor

- Spend less time at home and more time outside. When you are rich, stay at home more and less outside. When you are poor, spend money on others. When you're rich, spend money on yourself. Many people do the opposite.

- Be good to others. When you are rich, you must learn to let others be good to you. You have to learn to be better at being good to yourself.

- Throw yourself out in the open and let people make good use of you. When you are rich, you have to conserve yourself well and don't let people easily make use of you.

- You do not need to be afraid of being poor. You need to know how to invest in yourself and increase your wisdom and stature. When buying people dinner, make sure you buy dinners for people who have bigger dreams than you and work harder than you.

Lotus

According to a study by the University of Colorado, it's not the poorest countries sending people to the richest countries, it's countries in transition—still poor, but with some education and mobility—that are the highest migratory contributors. As countries develop, they continue to send more migrants, and at some point they become migrant-receiving regions themselves.

Russel Holding – a real multicultural

"I was born in London to an English dad and an Irish mom and brought up in Yorkshire. When I was 10 years old my parents moved to New Zealand as my dad got an opportunity to work on a dairy farm. I finished my schooling in New Zealand and then studied engineering in London. I worked in France and Belgium then moved to Hong Kong. My wife is Vietnam-born, brought up in Canada and when she was in her early twenties had migrated to Australia. We lived in Sydney for 6 years and then in early 2000 we moved to Melbourne.

"Though I am Caucasian and lived in Sydney, I felt a bit lonely. I found in Sydney they have an untold class culture; rich, middle class, poor people. You are rated by your material possession. I found a big barrier with Australians when it comes to interacting with Pommies. I didn't find Sydney very welcoming; Melbourne is much better. I found people do lots of socializing mostly based on common interests such as sports and clubs. I also got hooked up with people who are into music. Melbourne gave me that opportunity to play piano again after childhood. I composed my own music and played it on radio. I engaged myself with lots of community activities and voluntary works. Australia is a great country to do volunteer activities. When I go back to my country I find a reverse cultural effect and it's increasingly hard to relate to them. "

Lavender

In 2013, the number of international migrants was 232 million and is projected to double to over 400 million by 2050

- South-South: the largest flow of migrants, just over 82 million or 36 per cent in 2013.

- South-North: the second-largest flow, just under 82 million or 35 per cent, moved from a developing to an industrialized country.
- North-North: some 54 million people or 23 per cent of international migrants moved from one industrialized country to another.
- North-South: almost 14 million people or 6 per cent of migrants moved from industrialized to developing countries.

Jimmy Virago – from camp to corporate

Jimmy was born in Romania and lived there until he was 30 years old. He finished engineering while living with his parents and grandfather. Then the Romanian Revolution erupted—a series of riots and protests in Romania in December 1989. During that riot his grandfather and father were both killed.

He left Romania and literally fled to Germany to save his wife and himself. After a long 3 to 4 days without food and sleepless nights, he landed in East Berlin. Germany offered asylum rights to people fleeing from political persecution and provided financial aid. It was an amazing experience for him, living in German camps. In that situation of unrest where everything was controlled by the military or government, he wanted to get his freedom back so he migrated to Australia in 1991. Later he brought his mother and they all lived in Melbourne.

Jimmy said: "I always worked hard to prove my worth but I strongly believe that you need more than that to succeed in this society. You need to socialize, you need to spend time with locals and you need to understand the culture. I was busy with my professional life and chasing money and I gave a great education to my child but many times felt there is not much left for me. I am still rooted in Romania and an outsider to this country. Overall migration gave me freedom—the reason I was here in the first place—it gave me all the material stuff. Most migrants just focus only on money and material stuff—don't do that, life is much more beautiful and stress-free outside that. I always tell my son to live a stress-free happy life and listen to your heart as you already have freedom of choice."

Daisy

About 60 per cent of global migrants are in the 30 or more industrialized countries. Some 40 per cent of migrants are in the 170 poorer developing countries. Almost half of the world's migrants are women, 15 per cent of migrants are under 20, and less than 7 per cent of all international migrants are refugees.

Sudip Mishra – story about reverse culture shock

Sudip was born in India and migrated eight times in his life; five times within India and the remainder was inter-country. After living a couple of decades in Australia he took a one-year immersive cultural experience for his children and lived in India. Each time it was a huge cultural shock—a new language, places, faces, ways of doing things but within 3-6 months he was charmed by the new place and feeling that "indeed, the way they do things here is the best."

He tells the story: "Moving to Melbourne was a dream come true. The job I had at Andersen Consulting was exactly what I had dreamt of as an undergraduate at university. Moving to Hardwar for the one-year sabbatical was a wonderful experience in every sense—we travelled the length and breadth of the most beautiful country that India is. As a personal rule, I don't dwell on regrets and don't regard any setback as a "failure." I have a deep-seated belief in destiny and divine providence. Most people will agree that in hindsight, something that upset them greatly when it happened turned out to be the best possible thing that could have happened, as it pointed them to a new path or led them to a different journey.

"I feel I would score very highly on any adaptability, assimilation and socialization indices. I am an optimist and like to look for positives in any person or situation that I encounter, so that helps assimilate and adapt. My socialization is broad and mixed. It tends to be based around specific areas of interest. I have had the relative luxury of being a local graduate in Australia. It is now when I am in India and as I am trying to expand our business here that I am facing a reverse-migration challenge—of adapting to the Indian corporate work culture."

Gladiolus

Lifelong learning is a mindset. A lifelong learner:

- becomes more and more interesting and charismatic
- becomes more independent and well equipped
- always tries out new exciting things with full motivation and excitement
- asks more questions which lead to more information
- doesn't get stuck in a social situation becomes a better leader and earns more money

Joanna Mendez – passion follower

Joanna migrated with her parents in 1985 when she was 5-years-old from Ireland to Australia though originally they were from Mexico. This family lived in Australia for long enough, but when it came to parenting displayed a dominant parenthood style. Joanna was always absorbed in movies; she always loved activities like creative script writing, editing, make-up, and the special effects aspect of movies. For her, movies were not just fun or mere entertainment; the time devoted to watching movies was meant to be a learning experience. But as her parents were doctors they wanted her to pursue a career in the medical stream.

After finishing school with great results she got admission into medicine. She won university awards in those 4 years of studies in creative writing, portraying the role of Cleopatra and as a director for her drama play about mental health in an inter-university competition. For her tremendous passion and interest, her university sent her to Hollywood for an internship program with Kevin Spacey. She finished her education to become a doctor but with her engagement and passionate her potential was recognized and she got a chance to get into Hollywood. She finally decided to move to Hollywood to work on movie projects. Her latest update was that she was working for Pixar and was very happy.

Jasmine

Higher levels of migrant well-being can be instrumentally important for social outcomes as happier individuals are typically more productive and healthier. Migrant dissatisfaction may reflect social exclusion and a lack of assimilation, and even extremist attitudes among natives, all of which can result in social unrest and lower economic output. It is both parties' responsibility to look after each other—as we are all human and everything in the world is of the people, by the people, and for the people.

With "unity without uniformity and diversity without fragmentation" different cultural, linguistic, social, religious, political, ideological norms and perceptions really fabricate a beautiful bouquet.

CHAPTER 10

Clouds to My Sky

"Clouds come floating into my life, no longer to carry rain or usher storm, but to add color to my sunset sky."
Rabindranath Tagore

Like many other migrants I am fortunate to have migrated both inter- and intra- country and it has been an amazing journey. Born and brought up in a small township in the eastern part of India, I moved to metropolis Kolkata when I was 9. That was my first migration. Moving forward I migrated to the Gold Coast,

Australia when I was 23, then on to Sydney and Melbourne. Now after 15 years I feel local in Australia and get reverse culture shock in my home country. I should begin with a philosophy from George S. Patton, a US Army General - "I don't measure a man's success by how high he climbs but how high he bounces when he hits the bottom."

Two Sides of a Coin

In 1947, after the India-Pakistan (Bangladesh) partition, my grandfather migrated to India due to political unrest, with my grandmother and a handful of money. He became very successful and said, "There are two kinds of people who do business: one who can't get any another occupation and ends up doing any kind of business; and the other who just wants to do it because they love it." He always encouraged me and used to tell me, "You have to give people work." By 1965 he had already established a small scale factory with 25 employees and within a year initiated building a fabric processing factory, which eventually employed over 300 people.

My father who was good in academics, enrolled for an engineering degree. In the last year due to the Naxallite movement he couldn't finish his degree. He was a champion Bridge player and science fiction writer. He took over the family business and eventually his first silk processing unit accommodated more than 400 employees and he was quoted by the press as a next generation entrepreneur in the 80's.

In late 90's, factories had to shut down. As a typical father his entire attention was now focused that his only son would achieve everything he dreamt for. He was a strict and disciplined person but as I grew older, I started feeling a friend in him. He always encouraged me to meet and talk to people as much as possible, so that I could learn the skill of understanding people and grow my interpersonal skills. He supported me with my decision of migrating abroad.

My mother comes from a very settled, well known and big family. My grandfather, popular by his nickname 'Mana' was an ace right winger in the Mohanbugun Sporting Club. Named as 'Racing Deer' he later captained the team and was selected in 'Best Ever 11'. I loved their vibrant, sporty and carefree approach towards life alongside their passion, love and support.

As I go through this journey of writing about migrants, I can clearly visualize the two different approaches towards life. One side belonged to the migrant population for whom survival and establishment were the vital issues whereas the other side, since they were locally well-established, were more into prestige, respect and social status. That zeal to make it or break it was less in them, but it was compensated by their sense of belonging, love, care and community. Both sides wanted to succeed but their perception and strategies were different.

Go with the Flow. But ...

After finishing school in 1996 with a science stream, I decided to pursue mathematics honours with a plan to do a post-graduation in computer science later on. Since the IT industry had just started, great opportunities, attractive salaries and overseas projects were the main motivators. I have to agree that the education I had chosen soon started losing interest for not getting any practical relevance, just the unnecessary burden of theorems and formulas. Ultimately, my results were not up to the mark. The subject I took out of love rendered me penniless after 3 years.

After my honours I enrolled for a computer course and started preparing for the Masters in Computer Science entrance exam. My confidence was extremely low. I was searching for something new, challenging. In December 2000, a relative had visited Australia as a tourist. He insisted my father think about enrolling me in an Australian University. He said "I am sure he will find his own way."

I was thrilled with the idea, that I could go abroad, could start from scratch. I was focused, motivated, and energetic. In July 2001, I landed at Brisbane International Airport, all by myself, with lots of uncertainties in mind to start my new life in Australia. I was enrolled in a Masters in IT at Griffith University, Gold Coast.

Journey Begins ... Known to Unknown

Like other migrants my desire to achieve something big led me to overcome the pain of leaving my comfortable life behind. My father said some words just before I flew, "Think as if all doors in India are now closed for you, so, love the country, embrace it, mingle with the locals and live life in your own terms." Soon after, I was informed that I had also got through the admission test into one of the most prestigious institutes for MCA in India.

From the very first day, I promised myself that I would never discuss my struggle with my parents back in India, rather I will find someone here who can sort out the matter for me. I moved into a shared accommodation and became busier with university, studies, meeting new students and so on. Some of my friends had to start doing odd jobs immediately to support their studies. I was watchful, observing, trying to understand the system and gaining confidence. I was lucky enough to get initial support by my father, so didn't do any jobs in the first 6 months.

After a couple of months, I moved in with an Indian family as a paying guest. Initially it was good but within a couple of months our relationship started worsening. He was a violent alcoholic and had a bad name in the neighborhood (he was murdered a few years later). I started feeling restless. The whole situation was very scary for a 23-year-old newcomer. A couple of my friends let me move into their apartment. I started earning money from Call-Centre and dish washing jobs. After that I never had to ask for any money.

I tried to experience the country, mixing with new students, neighbors from other countries and involving myself in college activities. I never enjoyed technical classes but I enjoyed software quality management, planning, designing, scheduling and the projects. In our final semester we did a project on the International Student Association. On the first day, the course convener showed us a documentary about a high rise, explaining how the building would look in virtual reality, with the interiors and even the position of the pictures on the wall, whereas the digging hadn't even started. It blew my mind. He was not interested in our coding capability, he wanted to see our planning and scheduling. Someone had finally told me something I could really relate to. Though our coding didn't work in all the areas, the roadmap and planning documents we produced got our team a Distinction in the final project assessment. The insecurity I had that I don't like technicality was driven off by my keenness in planning.

Sharing my problems, confusions and seeking guidance to teachers or seniors were the only options I had, as I believed my friends were also having the same amount of experience and going through confusion. I was badly looking for a mentor. I could not find anyone. I started applying for jobs. The first big hurdle was I didn't have Permanent Residency (PR).I used to work 60 to 70 hours while waiting for my PR to save enough money so I could quit the odd jobs.

I always felt that just having a good job would not pay off my struggle. I don't want to be just an ordinary guy living in Australia. I wanted more rewards, something that I could not possibly achieve in India, something that the future generations would also benefit from, some legacy to leave behind. My odd jobs days taught me about the value of individuals, respect for a job and being professional. I always tried to help new students by giving shelter, with pickup and drop-off to work and university, giving referrals for odd jobs and so on.

Being to Becoming

I got my PR in January 2003. It was time for me to try something new, so odd jobs days were over. I had already realized there was not much opportunity on the Gold Coast and so made my move to Brisbane. With no luck in Brisbane, I moved to Sydney with savings of

$4000 and a hope to get a proper job in the IT sector.

Sydney was very different from the Gold Coast or Brisbane, so another phase of understanding the city and life started. With 3 months gone, without any job and my bank balance going down, I had to go back to factory cleaning. I quit after 4 weeks and got a job at a Call-Centre, where I could work up to 70 hours a week with a $16 an hour flat rate. I worked there till September 2003. I went to India for a year to settle down my mind and during this time, when I met my future wife.

In July 2004, I got married to Pallabi, a Bengali girl who mostly lived away from Bengal. Because of a military background moving from one city to another was a regular event for them. She had far more multicultural exposure than me. Girl Scouts to Zonal Level, playing volleyball at a national level gave her immense exposure about other dimensions of life. She lost her parents at an early age and because of that, her perception towards life is very bold, optimistic, and energetic. She always says "I have lost my parents, I have dealt with life without them, my future can't be worse than this." She is and has always been a big support and strength to me mentally and emotionally. She is involved in acting and with a dance group which performs professionally and also does shows to support charity work.

In September 2004 I returned to Sydney with $1500 in my bank account. My wife joined me in May 2005. These 8 months, I applied for thousands of jobs, but all I received responses for were Call-Centre jobs – no IT job came my way. I worked at a Call-Centre for 12 weeks to get some money rolling. I was $20,000 in debt to buy a car and to set up my new life. I wanted to live this honeymoon phase of life to the fullest.

In the second week of May, I went for an interview for a Call-Centre role. I laid my story on the table. The interviewer, after listening said she had a better job for me and offered me the role of Lending Officer at the National Australia Bank (nab). I was happy because it was a desk bound job. Within 6 months I became one of the best performers with 150% to 180% productivity. I helped 8 of my friends to get into nab in the same type of role. But soon it started to seem repetitive and I began to get bored because I wasn't learning anything new. I spoke to the management and they gave me an opportunity to get into the analyst team. In 2006, when nab started outsourcing, I realized there was no more growth there and it was the best time to move out. In January 2007, I decided to give it one last try to get into proper IT and started applying for jobs in the big companies throughout Australia. After living in Surfer's Paradise, Sydney felt very a busy and hectic city. I never liked Sydney – another reason being our inability to reside in the good suburbs. It took me 9 long months, and around 40-50 different interviews to finally get into that.

I moved to Melbourne to join Intergraph as a Program Analyst in the Asia Pacific team. With a great salary hike and opportunity to travel abroad and work all over the world. I was thrilled, happy and motivated again. Professionally it was a huge jump and socially Melbourne was much more welcoming. 3 months on, I was the Cultural Secretary in the Social Association of Victoria. We were personally close to nearly 100 established families by then.

This move was a great learning experience in all aspects of my career. From doing business analysis to travelling overseas to train engineers all over the world, I was enjoying every moment of it. Within 6 months, I was given an opportunity to choose either project management or to train in a product. My obvious choice was project management as it was more about dealing with people and an opportunity to get a whole view about business. All was going well until June 2008, when US management decided to dissolve the Asia Pacific team. I was made redundant in November 2008. In September 2008 we had our first child and my wife was on maternity leave.

First Year of Unemployment: 2008 – 2009

It took me 366 days to get my next job in project management, because that was what I wanted. I did not want to go back to odd jobs, just for finance sake. Australian social security helped me to keep my focus intact. I have always maintained a philosophy in life that the last thing I would compromise is the life and my family. I saw my child growing, starting to talk and crawling.

In December 2009, I joined Telstra as Project Coordinator and my wife also went back to work after maternity leave. I learned new systems, methods, processes, ideas, professionalism, and communication. I met great people with whom I could share and seek help. I impressed my team with my skills overall and within a year I was doing project management. My salary was doubled. There was a change in management in December 2010 and the whole chain of people I developed a rapport with had gone. The new GM didn't acknowledge my new role and I was demoted to Project Coordinator again with a lower salary, no growth and no learning.

My Vulnerable World

My previous boss in Telstra figured out that once I finished my learning, my passion and interest started fading. I will give a simple example: let's say I want to learn to cook Butter Chicken. I will do everything to learn that, will follow the procedure, and might improvise a bit to make it as close as possible to the recipe. My philosophy is I don't need to know exactly 100% of it, rather I will jump into learning to cook Biriyani or something else. Because perfection is an illusion and nothing is perfect.

Socializing is something I have always enjoyed, resulting in having a large group of friends. One of my very close friends in India was Arijit Sengupta who was a genius in mathematics and very knowledgeable. We used to discuss philosophy, psychology, religion, science, literature, theatre and many other things, which are still part of my passion and give me immense pleasure knowing more about them. In 2006 he died in an accident. He used to say, "Goutam, very few people actually live; and most of us just watch them and try to imitate that way of life. You have to live and we want to watch your living." I miss his company and his inspiration in many ways.

New learning, people, environment and challenges always drove me. I believe life and learning are joyfully synonymous and we shouldn't stop learning. In June 2011 I changed my job. I applied to many places but got another contract at Telstra. I joined Telstra IT. I never got a proper welcome, never understood people over there and ended up in a team lacking any aspiration, focus, motivation as they were insecure of losing their jobs. I came across narcissistic behavior in the people and management.

My wife was pregnant with our 2nd child. One fine morning suddenly a thought came to my mind; is my baby all right? What if it was disabled? It just drained me emotionally for the next 4-5 months. I did everything possible but this would not go away from my mind.

I am very friendly and used to hang around with lots of friends from different circles. I have never had bad experiences with friends. From mid-2011 my definition of friendship started changing, as in bad times people began showing their true colors. That also left me feeling very lonely. Our second daughter was born in January 2012 and I lost my job in April 2012. For the next year I worked only 12 weeks.

Lost Purpose and Direction

I kept thinking on would another job change my life? I didn't know which job to apply for. I didn't know what I would enjoy. I used to love socializing all the time. But now I liked to be by myself or with my family. I lost purpose. I lost direction.

As in the bad times a lot of people left my life (in a way it's good I believe now because they were not there for you) I should say a few people also pop into your life as a pillar, as support, as a guide. Because in that most vulnerable moment you can't really tolerate fake relations, fake smiles and superficial attachments.

I received support from Somyojyoti Banerjee a very close friend of mine in the form of a philosopher guide. We discuss a lot about the brain, mental power, philosophy of education, Hindu mythology, western civilization, technology for mankind, and humanity's understanding of real relationships. Hours and hours of discussion which were very mentally stimulating and I could be fully vulnerable in front of him. The whole discussion is to grow, to flourish with ideas, to understand the bigger picture. Now he lives in Sydney but we make time to talk and it's a need for us from a creativity perspective.

In your bleakest moment when it seems all doors are closing if you can strongly believe other doors are opening, life will allow that for you. And it's really true for all that happens in life there is a purpose.

I strongly believe that there are different ways you can help an individual and we did from time to time. Especially as a migrant, we help when someone is moving to a different city, moving property, referring someone to your job place to recruit, giving a new migrant initial shelter, introducing a newcomer to your circle, informing them about the norm of life in the new land and financially assisting. I believe this help is necessary but is the lowest and cheapest possible way to do that. Real help is if you can show someone direction in life, give inspiration to follow their heart or create a situation for them so that they can flourish in their own way.

I asked some of my colleagues and friends about my attributes because sometimes I thought I didn't have any skills. They tried to motivate me saying: I am extremely friendly, I can approach anyone without hesitation; I am quite emotional and can get hurt for trivial matters but that emotion can also bring passion and creativity to what I love to do; I have some hidden talent (for which field neither they nor myself know, but it's just their gut feeling); great communication skills; and I have good people skills that leads to very good leadership skills. I can establish trusted relationships with people, support them if necessary, pull the emotional strings and get the work done from them.

I always see myself as a guy running his own show, motivating thousands of people and making my mark in their minds. I can't just work for the sake of working. I want my work to mean something, to encourage people. I have quite a few well-wishers and a very supportive wife who always trusts me and believes I could do something big in life. But during this one year, I couldn't make any new friends, couldn't do anything new. Life was directionless, suffocating. Sometimes even my kids could not keep my spirits up. I ceased enjoying anything. I could feel my family was suffering for that as well, so I consulted a doctor and was declared clinically depressed and was on medication. I gradually calmed down, learnt different aspects of life and could sleep properly at night. Even after this, my desire to do something was still strongly there. Just to lead a normal risk free life is not enough. But I am happy with whatever I have.

New Perception, View ... Recovery

With my mind reeling in depression and unemployment, my days were turning into absolute nightmares. I had worked 14 different jobs in 7 different industries in the past 10 years. With intentions of starting my own business I started visiting several business forums from 2011. Meeting new people with an avalanche of new ideas in my head – the feeling was phenomenal. It was here that I met businessman Saurabh Mishra. He expressed his faith in me and encouraged me to try my hand at business. He suggested I go for a career counselling session. It was an amazing experience. The counsellor, Dale Simpson, pinpointed things my heart always wanted. His analysis was that I was a thorough people person, all about creativity, ideas and motivation.

One incident fresh in my memory is meeting Saurabh on 13 May 2013, at around 5pm at his office. I had been rejected in 3 interviews, was running a temperature and my kids were ill at home. I was mentally devastated. It was on that day that I decided never to work for someone again, to try my hand out at business, yet I had no formal experience in business. People posed questions about why business would come to me, what did I have to offer that other businessmen could not? I always believed and saw people do business on trust and relationship. I have full confidence that I can achieve that. Another businessman I met was Mario Misso who became my mentor, friend, guide and a father-figure in my journey as an entrepreneur.

I am a big fan of Sourav Ganguly, the ex-Captain for India. I admire his determination, vision and leadership skills. I like him because looking from a distance I strongly feel he had to reinvent himself again and again. Just like him, I believe that one person can truly help another to be inspired and fulfil their dreams. I play cricket with our social club here. After losing 14 matches in a row, it was decided that a new captain should be appointed to bring some freshness to the team and thus I was given the responsibility to lead the team. From the first day I took it very seriously, always taking pains to make sure the team was properly motivated. We won the next 9 matches. The most positive thing was that the team was always eager for the next match. I used to motivate the team with the line "We Will Win". Everybody gave their best every time, not only to win but also to have a good time. Everyone was proud of their own performances and I was proud of the team. We lost the final match but I was still satisfied that we had grown as a team, with proper unity and spirit.

My Entrepreneurial Journey: Infonity

"We Will Win" has become the statement of my life. I keep reminding this to myself and stay motivated. What I needed was a direction, a dream which would make life worth living again.

On 3rd June 2013, I registered my company, Infonity. All the pain, suffering and experiences I had gone through over the years are the seeds of Infonity. That is the reason why our tag line is: **Dream, Believe, Achieve**. I learnt from my family and my mentors that you can grow only when you help others to grow. I want to help people who have lost direction in their careers and help organizations to grow their business.

We are doing HR consulting because human resource is the heart and soul of any business. A resume can't flash out your attitude, thus do not understand dreams and zeal of the person. We also do recruitment; we are specialised in Workforce Diversity and Mental Health Consulting for organizations and governments. We also started an IT consultancy as Infonity Solutions where we are working with the latest technologies. Along the way we developed two

E-Learning Products on Diversity and Mental Health. Currently we are operating nationally in Australia. In March 2014 Infonity started operations in India, focusing on early intervention on mental health. In this journey I met an author, speaker and researcher about brain and body Dr Siddhartha Ganguly in India who motivated me to write.

On this journey, I continue to meet like-minded people. I have been able to remove all outer world motivation from my life. I am trying to spend every moment where I am learning or enriching myself. If you measure success with money (which you should not be), then I am yet to reach the high flying league, but my belief gets stronger every day. More that we have more we can share and help. I can feel my dream is getting clearer, I work with greater passion and focus and more so a meaningful, calm and peaceful state of mind.

According to Sadhguru, fulfilment does not come because of some action you perform. Only if your inner nature is complete, will your life attain fulfilment. You are getting stressed out simply because you don't know how to function smoothly within yourself. You have no control over your own system. If your mind, body and energies were taking instructions from you and behaving the way you wanted them to, you wouldn't get stressed no matter what was happening around you. You will continue living life by accident. So equip yourself to make yourself the way you want to be. How vibrant and focused your mind is, how vibrant and healthy your body is, that's what decides how successful you are.

Life is fun and I am happy … and I know it will improve more and more.

"Happiness is when what you think, what you say, and what you do are in harmony."
Mahatma Gandhi

References

YouTube and other media offer a wealth of information. Annual reports published by various global organisations such as PWC, Deloitte, KPMG, Bersin, Government Departments, WHO etc. Here's a selection of what I watch online: TED talks, Oprah Winfrey, Sadhguru, Sri Sri Ravi Shankar, Swami Sarvapriyananda, Bill Gates, Steve Jobs, Seth Godin, John Maxwell, Dalai Lama, Ken Robinson, Eckhart Tolle, Thomas Sowell, Dr Wayne Dyer, Tony Robbins, Deepak Chopra, B M Hegde, Salman Akhtar, Dr Colin Ross, Dr Dinesh Bhugra, Dr Vikram Patel, BBC, National Geography.

http://www.multiculturalaustralia.edu.au/

https://www.dss.gov.au/

www.unaa.org.au

www.dca.org.au

https://www.humanrights.gov.au

www.mentalhealthvic.org.au

https://mhsa.aihw.gov.au

www.mentalhealthcommission.gov.au

https://www.beyondblue.org.au

www.blackdoginstitute.org.au

https://www.psychologytoday.com/

www.psychology.com

www.apa.org

www.forbes.com

www.harvard.edu

https://en.wikipedia.org/wiki

http://www.artofliving.org/knowledge-sheets

www.psychology.org.au

www.ishafoundation.org

http://bmhegde.com

http://joshbersin.com

www.bersin.com

http://www.oecd.org

http://www.renewoureconomy.org

http://www.pwc.com

"Intellectuals and Society" - Thomas Sowell

"Immigration and Identity" - Salman Akhtar

"The Cultural Intelligence Difference" - David A. Livermore

"Awaken The Giant Within" - Tony Robbins

"Emotional Intelligence and Diversity" - Gardenswartz, Lee, Jorge Cherbosque, Anita Rowe

"Essential Wisdom From A Spiritual Master" – Sadhguru

"The Mystic Eye" – Sadhguru

"Adversity Quotient: Turning Obstacles Into Opportunities" - Paul Stoltz

"Creative Schools: The Grassroots Revolution That's Transforming Education" - Ken Robinson and Lou Aronica

"The Moral Molecule" - Paul J. Zak

"Authentic Happiness" - Martin Seligman

"What Color Is Your Parachute?" - Richard Nelson

About the Author

Born in 1977, Goutam considers himself as Mathematics Honours and Masters in Information Technology by education, entrepreneur by logic, egalitarian by heart, life and learning are joyfully synonymous by attitude.

Author of "Jailbreak : Unblock the friend within to conquer this big small world", instructor of two e-learning products and migrated four times so far both inter-country and intra-country.

After many years understanding to assimilate in different places, he has gone on to found successful consultancy company, Infonity *(www.infonity.com.au)*. They are in HR consulting, recruitment and human analytics. They are also specialised in Workforce Diversity and Mental Health Consulting for organizations and governments. Infonity also started an IT consultancy as Infonity Solutions where they are working with the latest technologies and along the way they developed two E-Learning Products on

Diversity and Mental Health. Currently they are operating nationally in Australia. In March 2014 Infonity started operations in India, focusing on early intervention on mental health.

Vast experience from his early odd jobs to established corporate roles in several IT companies has sown the seeds for writing this book. He worked in 14 jobs in 7 different industries has given him invaluable experience in understanding how migrants and locals think and act. He exemplifies the expression "from nothing to everything" and is currently settled in Melbourne, Australia. Always a people person, his natural ease at socializing and attitude of taking risks, led him to turn to business, as did his apathy towards working for other people. With a great vision to operate business globally already in its third year, Infonity has created strong buzz in the business community.

Contact : *goutam.basak@infonity.com.au*

NOTES

_____

_____

_____

_____

_____

_____

_____

_____

_____

_____

_____

_____

_____

_____

_____

_____

_____

_____

_____

_____

_____

_____

NOTES